The Discovery
of South America
and the Andalusian Voyages

Louis-André Vigneras

The Discovery
of South America
and the Andalusian Voyages

Published for The Newberry Library by
The University of Chicago Press
Chicago and London

Louis-André Vigneras, who retired from the faculty of George
Washington University in 1968, has contributed articles to the
New England Quarterly, the *Hispanic American Historical Review,*
Imago Mundi, Terrae Incognitae, the *Revista de Indias,* and other
journals. In 1960 the Orion Press and the Hakluyt Society published
his revised translation of Columbus' *Journal.*

E
121
V53

The University of Chicago Press, Chicago 60637
The University of Chicago Press, Ltd., London

© 1976 by The University of Chicago
All rights reserved. Published 1976
Printed in the United States of America

Library of Congress Cataloging in Publication Data

Vigneras, Louis-André, 1903–
    The discovery of South America and the Andalusian
voyages.

    (Studies in the history of discoveries)
    Bibliography: p.
    Includes index.
    1. America—Discovery and exploration.   I.
Title   II. Series.
E121.V53   980'.01   75–19505
ISBN 0–226–85609–7

CONTENTS

PREFACE

In 1825, an officer in the Spanish Navy, Martin Fernández de Navarrete, began the publication of his *Colección de Viajes*, the first comprehensive study of the discovery of America. It dealt with Columbus, the "Minor Voyages," Vespucci and Magellan. Since then, Columbus, Vespucci and Magellan have been the objects of numerous studies. New documents have been found and thoroughly scrutinized, giving rise to new interpretations by some of the best brains on both sides of the Atlantic.

Not so with the Minor, or Andalusian Voyages, that followed Columbus' discovery of South America in 1498. They have been largely neglected. Yet they revealed the existence of a continuous coastline from the Brazilian Elbow to Panama, and they paved the way for the conquest and colonization of Venezuela and Colombia and for the discovery of the Pacific. Their leaders helped lay the foundations of the Spanish Empire in South America.

To be sure, there have been articles, chapters, and books written on the Andalusian Voyages; but on the main their authors have just repeated Navarrete, without making much effort to find new material, so that, 150 years later, Navarrete is still considered the best source of information.

Since I retired from teaching in 1968, a great part of my time has been devoted to the preparation of this book. I have searched for new material in the Spanish archives, especially in the Archivo de Protocolos in Seville. The registers of these notarial archives contain a tremendous wealth of documents: contracts between the leaders of the voyages and bankers, merchants, shipowners, and mariners; leases, loans, promissory notes, powers of attorney, investors' meetings, wills, summonses, sales of Indian slaves. This has made it possible for me to enlarge Navarrete's study by adding some voyages which had been virtually unknown, such as the Vélez de Mendoza—Luis Guerra expedition of 1500–1501. A fascinating character this Alonso Vélez de Mendoza, Commander of the Order of Santiago, poor as a church mouse. He had probably mortgaged his commandery and was always in debt. He looks like the predecessor of those penniless and famished hidalgos who grace the pages of *Lazarillo de Tormes, Alonso mozo de muchos amos* and other picaresque novels of the sixteenth and seventeenth centuries. Still, in the midst of adversity, he maintains his dignity.

Because of the nature of the newly found material, I have been able to bring to light economic factors that up to now have been neglected, particularly the leading role played by the merchants of Seville in financing such voyages, individually or through the constitution of companies. This does not apply only to the three wealthiest groups in the city: the Genoese, the bankers, and the *traperos* (drapers or cloth dealers); but also to men of different professions and walks of life: barbers, *bizcocheros*, blacksmiths, booksellers, etc. One family of *bizcocheros* deserves a special mention: the three brothers Guerra, Antón Marino, Luis, and Cristóbal, whose ancestral home was in Triana, in the Santa Ana parish. They made flour and *bizcocho* (hardtack) for the crews, and their family business prospered as naval trade increased. They contributed to the Andalusian Voyages not only with their money, but also with their persons, since they took part in five expeditions to the New World between 1498 and 1504. A preliminary study of their activities has already appeared in the *Hispanic American Historical Review* (November 1972).

If I am using the term "Andalusian" to refer to the voyages of Hojeda, Bastidas, La Cosa, the brothers Guerra, etc., it is because modern Spanish historians tend to do so. They feel that the epithet "Minor" applied to such undertakings by Navarrete minimizes their importance. In a recent letter to me, Professor Francisco de Solano makes the following comment about the "Minor" Voyages: "Why Minor? A cliché, and not a happy one to be sure." I agree with him, and he and my other Spanish friends will be glad to know that I have changed the name. Moreover, all these voyages originated in Andalusia. They sailed from Seville, from the Puerto de Santa Maria (in Cadiz Bay), or from Palos and Moguer, on the Rio Tinto.

I could not have brought this study to its successful conclusion without the collaboration of the staff members of the archives and libraries where I did my research: the Archivo General de Simancas, the Museo Naval in Madrid, the Archivo General de Indias, the Archivo Municipal de Sevilla, and the Archivo de Protocolos de Sevilla. To these should be added the National Geographic Society, the Folger Shakespeare Library, and the Library of Congress. Among the individuals whose aid and advice have been most helpful to me, I wish to single out Professor Antonio Muro Orejón, Professor Juan Collantes de Terán, Herr Doktor Klaus Wagner, and Don Juan Criado, all four expert paleographers, who have helped me solve a number of difficult readings in the Seville archives. In this country, I am indebted to Admiral Samuel Eliot Morison for his interest in my study and for suggesting that I put it into book form. Dr. Wilcomb Washburn (Smithsonian Institution), Dr. David Woodward (Newberry Library), and Professor John H. Parry (Harvard University) have examined my manuscript and paved the way for its publication. My nephew Professor William Duiker, Jr., of Pennsylvania State College, smoothed out a number of rough spots in my style, and his sister Miss Mary Duiker, of the National Geographic Society, helped draw some of the maps. To them and to others I express my gratitude. But for whatever defects and errors this book still contains, I alone am responsible.

Washington, D.C.
February 1975

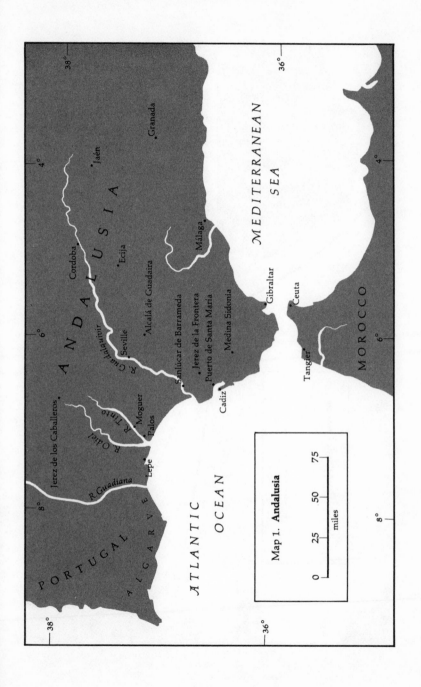

Map 1. **Andalusia**

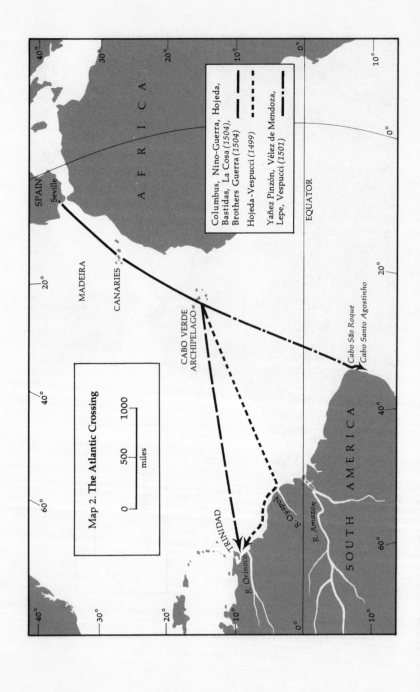

Map 2. The Atlantic Crossing

Columbus, Nino–Guerra, Hojeda,
Bastidas, La Cosa (1504),
Brothers Guerra (1504)

Hojeda–Vespucci (1499)

Yañez Pinzón, Vélez de Mendoza,
Lepe, Vespucci (1501)

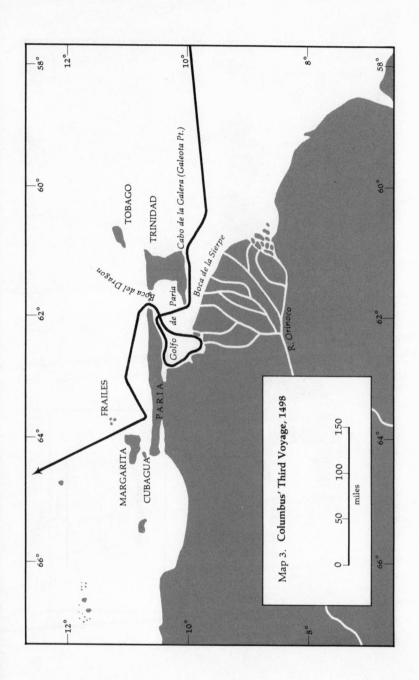

Map 3. Columbus' Third Voyage, 1498

TOBAGO

TRINIDAD

Cabo de la Galera (Galeota Pt.)

Boca del Dragón

Boca de la Sierpe

Golfo de Paria

R. Orinoco

FRAILES

PARIA

MARGARITA

CUBAGUA

miles

0   50   100   150

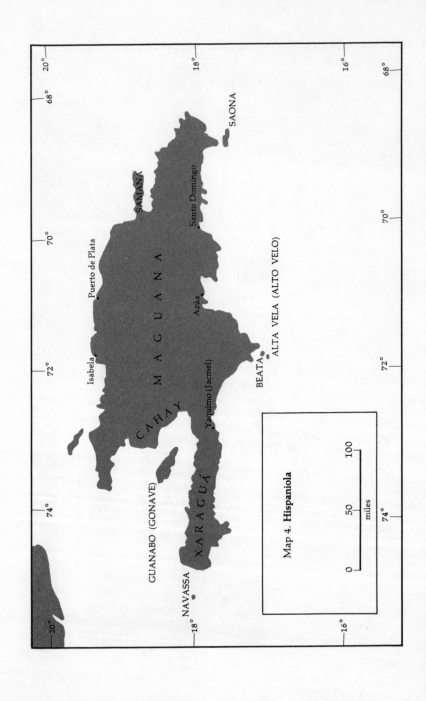

Map 4. **Hispaniola**

GUANABO (GONAVE)

NAVASSA

XARAGUÁ

C A H A Y

Isabela

Puerto de Plata

Yaquimo (Jacmel)

M A G U A N A

SAMANÁ

Azúa

Santo Domingo

SAONA

BEATA

ALTA VELA (ALTO VELO)

miles

0   50   100

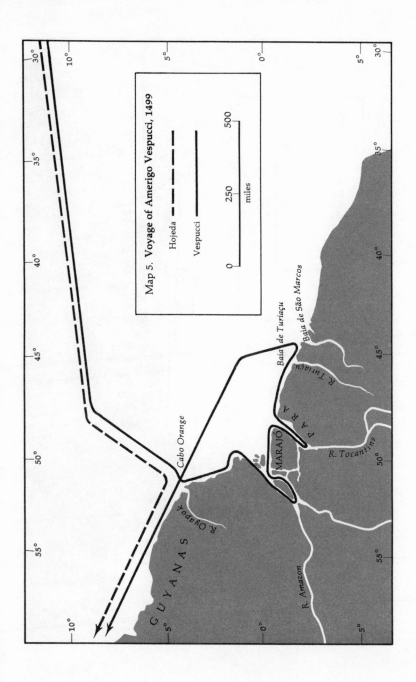

Map 5. Voyage of Amerigo Vespucci, 1499

Hojeda

Vespucci

0   250   500
miles

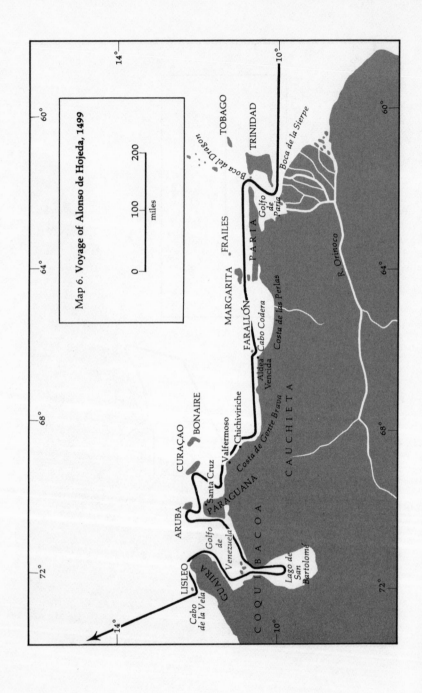

Map 6. **Voyage of Alonso de Hojeda, 1499**

0   100   200
miles

14°
60°
64°
68°
72°
14°

LISLEO
Cabo de la Vela
GUAIRA
COQUIBACOA
Golfo de Venezuela
Lago de San Bartolomé
10°
72°

ARUBA
CURAÇAO
BONAIRE
Santa Cruz
PARAGUANA
Valfermoso
Chichiviriche
Costa de Gente Brava
CAUCHIETA
68°

MARGARITA
FRAILES
FARALLÓN
Aldea Vencida
Cabo Codera
Costa de las Perlas
PARIA
Golfo de Paria
R. Orinoco
64°

TOBAGO
TRINIDAD
Boca del Drago
Boca de la Sierpe
10°
60°

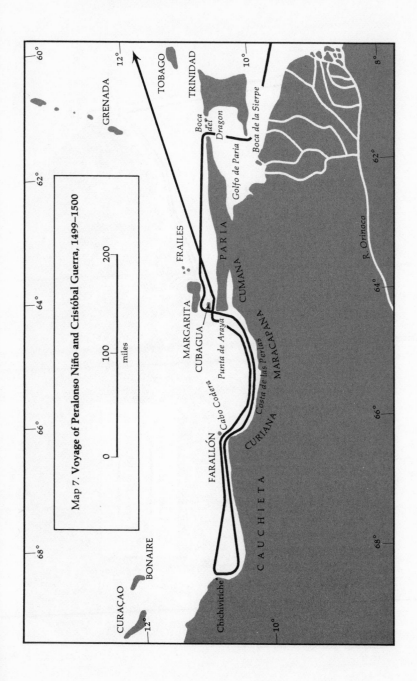

Map 7. **Voyage of Peralonso Niño and Cristóbal Guerra, 1499–1500**

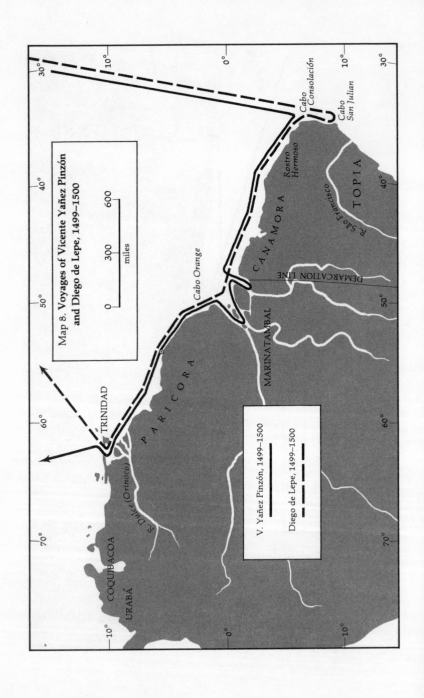

Map 8. Voyages of Vicente Yañez Pinzón and Diego de Lepe, 1499–1500

0   300   600

miles

V. Yañez Pinzón, 1499–1500 ——————

Diego de Lepe, 1499–1500 — — — —

COQUIBACOA

URABÁ

R. Dulce (Orinoco)

TRINIDAD

PARICORA

Cabo Orange

MARINATAMBAL

CANAMORA

Rostro Hermoso

Cabo Consolación

Cabo San Julian

TOPIA

R. São Francisco

DEMARCATION LINE

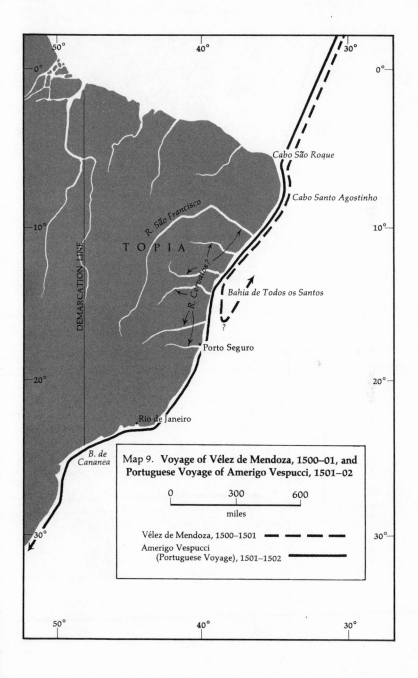

50° 40° 30°

0° 0°

Cabo São Roque

Cabo Santo Agostinho

R. São Francisco

10° TOPIA 10°

R. Cervatos?

Bahia de Todos os Santos

DEMARCATION LINE

?

Porto Seguro

20° 20°

Rio de Janeiro

B. de
Cananea Map 9. Voyage of Vélez de Mendoza, 1500–01, and
Portuguese Voyage of Amerigo Vespucci, 1501–02

0 300 600

miles

Vélez de Mendoza, 1500–1501 ━ ━ ━

Amerigo Vespucci
(Portuguese Voyage), 1501–1502 ━━━

30° 30°

50° 40° 30°

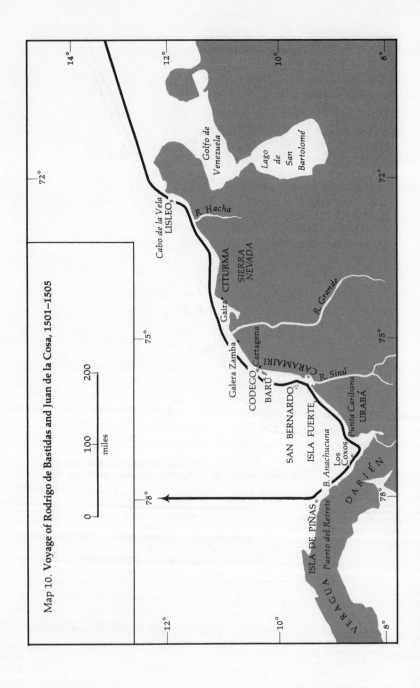

Map 10. Voyage of Rodrigo de Bastidas and Juan de la Cosa, 1501–1505

Cabo de la Vela
LISLEO
R. Hacha
Golfo de Venezuela
Lago de San Bartolomé
SIERRA NEVADA
CITURMA
Gaira
Galera Zamba
Cartagena
CODEGO
BARÚ
CARAMAIRI
R. Grande
R. Sinú
SAN BERNARDO
ISLA FUERTE
Punta Caribana
URABÁ
B. Anachucuna
Los Coxos
DARIÉN
ISLA DE PIÑAS
Puerto del Retrete
VERAGUA

0   100   200
miles

14°
12°
10°
8°
72°
75°
78°

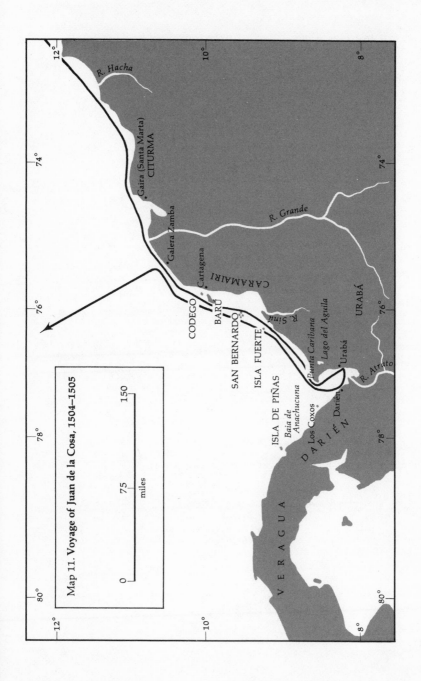

Map 11. Voyage of Juan de la Cosa, 1504–1505

miles

0   75   150

R. Hacha

Gaira (Santa Marta)
CITURMA

Galera Zamba

Cartagena

CODEGO

BARÚ

SAN BERNARDO

ISLA FUERTE

CARAMAIRI

R. Grande

R. Sinú

Punta Caribana

Lago del Aguila

URABÁ

Urabá

R. Atrato

ISLA DE PIÑAS

Baía de
Anachucuna

Los Coxos

Darién

DARIÉN

VERAGUA

1   The Discovery of South America
     by Columbus:
     Its Causes and Consequences

The Islands of Antilla

Christopher Columbus returned from his second voyage on 11 June
1496, and spent the next two years in Spain. He wanted to go back
as soon as possible, but no money was available for him, because the
Catholic Sovereigns were marrying two of their children to the son
and daughter of the emperor Maximilian. On 3 April 1497, amidst
the most extravagant pomp and splendor, Columbus attended the
wedding of the heir to the throne, Prince Juan of Spain, to Margaret
of Burgundy; but the joy and great expectations aroused by this union
soon turned to grief and sorrow, for the too happily married young
prince died six months later. For the Admiral (Columbus), 1497
was also a year of mixed feelings. He had been most honorably
welcomed by the rulers of Spain at his arrival; but he had come empty-
handed, without gold and without spices. Moreover, he could not
help but hear the ugly rumors that were spread around him. He
claimed he had reached Japan and China; but his detractors denied
it, asserting that the islands he had discovered were those of Antilla,
the legendary archipelago which appeared on fifteenth century
portolan charts and was also called the Seven Cities. The Florentine
cosmographer Toscanelli put it halfway between the Iberian
peninsula and Asia; and so did Martin Behaim on the globe he made
in Nuremberg in 1492.[1]

As early as November 1493, the chronicler Pietro Martire
d'Anghiera reported in his *Decades*: "He [Columbus] says that he
has discovered the Isle of Ophir, but if we take into account the
teachings of the cosmographers, those islands are the Antillas and
other adjacent ones."[2] Other individuals expressed the same opinion.
The Florentine Giovanni Strozzi, writing from Cadiz in March 1494,
announced the safe arrival of twelve caravels from the islands discovered by Columbus in the following terms: ". . . they have come in
twenty-five days from these Islands of Antilla."[3] To counter such
disbelief, after his exploration of the south coast of Cuba, Columbus

made his crew swear before a notary that Cuba was not an island, but part of the continent (*tierra firme*); and he threatened those who reneged with 10,000-maravedis fines (approximately $130 in today's currency) and with having their tongues cut out. "He might make everyone swear under dreadful penalties that Cuba was a peninsula of Asia and the Grand Khan just around the corner, that did not make it so."[4] He had an argument with the abbot of Lucena, "bono astronomo et cosmografo," Columbus maintaining that he had reached Asia, the other denying it. Fearing that the abbot's report to the Queen might be damaging and would hurt his credit, the Admiral did his best to keep him from returning to Spain.[5] But this scepticism was not confined to men of learning; it was shared by a number of merchants and sailors as well. In some commercial contracts and promissory notes preserved in the 1497 register of the notary Juan Ruiz de Porras, the West Indies are called "las islas de Antilla." Columbus himself is referred to in a document as "almirante del mar oceano de las yndias de Antilla."[6]

After the celebration of the princely weddings, the Admiral was able to plan his return to Hispaniola. Fernando and Isabel appropriated some funds toward the outfitting of a fleet of six vessels which was to transport troops, emigrants and supplies. Three hundred and thirty persons, picked by Columbus, were to go to the Indies: 40 *escuderos* (gentlemen), 100 foot soldiers, 30 able seamen or mariners, 30 apprentice seamen, 20 gold miners, 50 farmers, 10 gardeners, 20 artisans and 30 women (one woman for every 10 men!). They were to remain in the Indies as long as the Admiral felt they would be needed. They were to be paid by the Crown (except the women, who were expected to earn their way) at salaries varying according to categories, the highest paid being the escuderos, the able seamen, and the artisans, who were to get 30 maravedis a day, while the least favored were the farmers and the gardeners whose annual pay was to be 6,000 maravedis. In addition, everyone, including the 30 women, was to receive 12 maravedis a day for six months as maintenance.

To stimulate emigration, another *real cédula* (royal decree) offered royal pardon to all criminals willing to spend one or two years at their own cost in the Indies, with the exception of those accused of heresy, lèse-majesty, treason, murder, sodomy, and counterfeiting. This meant that jailbirds and other undesirable elements were encouraged to go to

Hispaniola, where they were expected to support themselves working in the mines.[7] Some priests and monks, a physician, an apothecary, and an herborist were also supposed to join the expedition.

There was also a provision for the shipping of tools, plows, grinding stones and other agricultural implements, and for the transport of twenty teams of cows, mares, burros, to pull the plows, carry packs, and produce offspring. Bulls and stallions are not mentioned, but some must have been included. Clothing also figured prominently in the list of supplies.[8]

Naturally, the chief item to be loaded on the Admiral's caravels was food. The settlers of Hispaniola were not expected to be self-supporting, being presumably too busy looking for gold to do much farming. They had to be provided with wheat, meat, wine, and oil from the home country. Supplying this food, shipping it, and distributing it in Hispaniola required a rich, capable, and relatively honest man, a rare species just as difficult to encounter in 1497 as it is today. And if such a man could be found, his assignment would be greatly hampered by the rapacity of the Seville merchants, who hid their merchandise and refused to sell it, waiting for an increase in the prices, in spite of government regulations against inflation and price gouging. The rulers of Spain had ordered Columbus and Antonio de Torres to find the indispensable person for that arduous task, which included providing 550 *cahices* (10,400 bushels) of wheat, 50 *cahices* (950 bushels) of barley, and 1,000 quintals (50 tons) of *bizcocho* (hardtack). No one was interested, however, because the Crown's purchase price was considered too low. Realizing this after seven months, the government raised its offer; Columbus and Bishop Juan Rodríguez de Fonseca, one of the Queen's most trusted advisors, were asked to try again (23 December 1497).[9] This time, they were successful in finding a qualified man willing to assume the responsibility for such a task, in the person of one Antón Mariño, a wealthy merchant who lived in Triana, in the Santa Ana parish.

Antón Mariño was the son of Diego Guerra and Beatriz Mariño. He had adopted his mother's maiden name, a fairly common practice of the time. He was a *bizcochero,* like his brother Luis, like his sister Beatriz, like his nephew Alonso de Monroy. As such, he made *bizcocho* and flour for the fleets going to England, Flanders, the Canaries, and Hispaniola. He appears for the first time in 1497 in the *Libros de*

Armada, where we learn that he received from the Spanish authorities 25 *cahices* (475 bushels) of wheat, which he turned into 200 quintals of *bizchocho,* receiving for his work 300 maravedis per *cahiz,* a total of 7,500 maravedis. The hardtack was for the two caravels of Pero Ferrández Coronel, which sailed for Santo Domingo on 23 January 1498.[10]

The hardtack business prospered over the years as naval trade increased, and it must have brought Antón Mariño considerable profit, for he was a man of means. Toward the end of 1497, he was approached by Columbus and Fonseca, who were acting in the name of the Crown, and on 1 January 1498, he signed a contract with them. By its terms, he was to buy a considerable amount of food supplies, load them at his own cost on five of the six ships which were to sail with the Admiral in the spring, and sell them to the settlers of Hispaniola at prices previously agreed on with the government (wine at 15 maravedis per *azumbre* or half-gallon, salt meat at 8 maravedis per pound, etc.). These prices were so calculated as to allow him a fair profit.[11] As a guarantee that he would fulfill his contract, Antón pledged all his worldly goods, his bondsman being Rodrigo de Gallegos, a relative and a member of the local gentry. Three weeks later (22 January), in the family home which was next to the Santa Ana church, Antón's wife Inez Nuñez pledged her dowry and her share of the family fortune, renouncing the clauses that in Roman Law protected married women.[12] The Crown lent Antón two thirds of the funds, the other third being provided by him. In all, he loaded 372 tons of merchandise, of which 252 were paid for by the government, and 120 with his own money. He also provided one third of the funds needed for the freighting of the five caravels, for the *averia* (insurance), and for four months' advance pay for the pilots.[13]

During the first five months of 1498, Antón took an active part in outfitting the fleet, and at various times we find him acting as paymaster. The armada sailed on 30 May. It consisted of six ships. Mariño went in the vessel commanded by Juan Antonio Colombo, the Admiral's cousin, and had charge of feeding the *escuderos* or "gentlemen" who were on board. These *escuderos* were an odd lot of officials, merchants, mining experts, and protégés of Columbus or of the Crown. Antón was classified as one of them; as such he collected 30 maravedis a day until his return to Spain in December. He was the first of the three Guerra brothers to set foot on American soil.

When the armada reached the Canaries, Columbus divided it. He sent three vessels directly to Hispaniola, and with the other three, he set sail for the Cabo Verde archipelago. He had decided to postpone his return to Santo Domingo and go south in search of a continent below the West Indies.

John Cabot

Why did the Genoese decide to steer southwest in search of land? The reason he gave was that the late King João II of Portugal had said that a *tierra firme* (landmass) might be found in that direction. João may well have made such a statement, since he was interested in discovery. According to an inscription on Martin Behaim's globe, he had ordered his subjects to undertake a search for "land beyond Ptolemy's description," that is, land not pictured in Ptolemy's *Geographia*. In this work, recently printed in Latin translation, the globe was described as tripartite, consisting only of three continents (Europe, Asia, Africa), and its habitable part was confined to the temperate zone.[14] It is true that João II had rejected the project submitted to him by Columbus, probably for financial reasons; but he had authorized Fernão Dulmo, a Flemish settler in Terceira (Azores) to search for land across the Atlantic *a sua costa* (at his own cost). This expedition does not seem to have materialized, since Dulmo was involved in litigation concerning land grants in Terceira Island and was called to Lisbon to help settle it, at about the time he had been expecting to sail on his voyage of discovery.[15]

Personally, I believe that the main reason why Columbus decided to investigate the possible existence of a *tierra firme* south of the West Indies was the recent discovery of a continent in the North Atlantic by John Cabot, an Italian in the service of Henry VII, King of England. Another inducement may have been a letter from the jeweler Jaime Ferrer (see p. 12).

John Cabot sailed from Bristol with some twenty men on a ship called the *Matthew*, about 20 May 1497. They struck land on 24 June, spent about a month exploring the coast, and were back in Bristol before 10 August, after making the return trip in only two weeks. Cabot claimed that he had discovered a new continent, which he called *Brasil,* or *Seven Cities,* stretching from the latitude of Bordeaux (45°N.) to that of Dursey Head (52°N.). Hence, it included Nova Scotia and Newfoundland. The name "Brasil" had nothing to do with dyewood; it is an Irish word meaning "happy," "blessed," and it was given to a mythical island situated on the Bristol parallel, west of Ireland, and pictured on maps since 1325. In addition, Cabot told the English king that the coast he had discovered was part of the land of the Grand Khan, where silk and spices were produced. On his next voyage, he would go further south, opposite the island of *Cipangu* (Japan), and found there a colony where from all these valuable products would be shipped to England, and he promised to turn London into a bigger spice emporium than Alexandria. No doubt, such glittering prospects made Henry's mouth water, to the point that the usually thrifty monarch granted him an annual pension and authorized him to sail again with six ships to the land discovered the year before (3 February 1498).[16]

The news of Cabot's discovery quickly spread over Western Europe, through ambassadors of various countries and foreign merchants, mostly Italian, who were doing business in England. The two nations most concerned were naturally Spain and Portugal, since they had already divided among themselves the undiscovered world through a vertical partition line 370 leagues west of the Cabo Verde archipelago, at a longitude of about 46° W. Each of these two countries was also trying to find its own route to India and the Land of Spices, the Portuguese making their way down the coast of Africa and around the Cape of Good Hope, while the Spaniards, led by Columbus, hoped to find such a route through the West Indies.

Cabot's voyage aroused much interest in Portugal, because, according to his own calculations, the land he had reached was within the zone assigned to Portugal by the treaty of Tordesillas (1494). Cabot had figured that the land in question was only 1,800 Roman miles from Europe. This many Roman miles was equivalent to 1,440 nautical miles. Since the distance between Ireland and Cape Race is 2,050 nautical miles, Cabot's error amounted to 600 miles. Of course, in those days, there was no adequate means of calculating the longitude. Furthermore, his error might be explained by the fact that on his return trip, with favorable winds behind him, he had covered the distance from Newfoundland to Europe in only two weeks.

The reaction to Cabot's voyage was probably the cause of the order that the Lusitanian monarch Dom Manoel (1495–1521) gave his navigators, to search for land across the Atlantic. That this order was successfully carried out we know from a passage of Duarte Pacheco Pereira, in his work entitled *Esmeraldo de situ orbis*, composed between 1505 and 1508. Here is the passage in question: "Fortunate Prince, we know and we have seen how, in the third year of your reign, in the year of our Lord 1498, Your Highness ordered us to discover the occidental part, beyond the ocean sea, where was found a huge continent surrounded by many large islands . . ."[17]

The search for land ordered in 1498 by Dom Manoel refers to the undertakings of the Terceiran navigators Pero de Barcelos, João Fernandes Labrador, and Gaspar Cortereal. We have proof of this in the Cantino map, drawn in 1502, the first map to picture the Portuguese discoveries in the north and to show the partition line. Next to Newfoundland is written the following legend: "This land was discovered by order of the most excellent Prince, Dom Manoel, King of Portugal. It was found by Gaspar Cortereal."

Nevertheless, we cannot overlook the possibility that Manoel's order applied to South America as well; for Alvares Cabral's landstrike on the east coast of Brazil can hardly be explained away as purely fortuitous.

John Day's Letter

The Spanish Court also showed keen interest in John Cabot's activities, and it was kept informed by its ambassadors in London, Pero de Ayala and Ruy González de la Puebla. The big concern was the voyage planned for 1498 and the direction it would take. "The route they are following leads to the possessions of Your Highnesses," wrote Pedro de Ayala from London in July 1498.[18] Still, the man best informed in

Spain about Cabot's discovery was Columbus himself, through a letter received from an English friend named John Day.

John Day was a Bristol merchant who traded in Spain. Documents from the Archivo de Protocolos in Seville show that he was in that city and in Sanlúcar de Barrameda in 1499. On 9 October, in Sanlúcar, he gave power of attorney to "Pedro Albordin [Alberdeen?] inglés, mi fator, vecino de la villa de Bristol:" and, by virtue of that power, some eighteen months later, Albordin settled a debt of 537,840 maravedis, which Day had owed to Batista Negrón and Francisco Pinelo, both members of the large Genoese colony in Seville. As a guarantee for the payment of his debt, John Day had pawned a large stock of English cloth which had been deposited in the care of Sebastian Doria. When Albordin paid back the sum, on 30 March 1501, the stock of cloth was turned over to him, and he and Sebastian Doria exchanged receipts.[19]

John Day did not deal in cloth exclusively; he was also interested in metals. This we know from a *real cédula*, which is kept in the Archivo de Simancas. On 20 December 1500, the Catholic Sovereigns ordered that 117 quintals and 82 pounds of lead be delivered to "Roberto Expexforte [sic] inglés . . . en nombre de Juan Day inglés." The 117 quintals and 82 pounds were equivalent to a cargo of lead belonging to John Day, which had been requisitioned the year before by Juan Gaytán, corregidor of Malaga, for the Moors in Alpujarra had rebelled, and the Spanish artillery was short of ammunition.[20]

John Day's real name was Hugh Say. He belonged to a prominent London family of wealthy merchants and members of Parliament, and he was related by marriage to Lord Mountjoy, Master of the Mint. In his business deals in Bristol, however, Hugh Say called himself John Day. On 10 May 1494, "John Day of London, merchant" was admitted into the membership of the Bristol Staple by payment of a large fee. Before that, he was already doing business in Bristol: local customs accounts for 1492–1493 show him importing wine and olive oil from Lisbon. In 1502–1503, he was involved in lawsuits with some Bristol merchants. Records of the testimonies given in Chancery Court reveal that "John Day now calling himself Hugh Say" had been actively engaged in the Anglo-Spanish trade. He was still alive in December 1517, when he made his will, styling himself "late of London, mercer, now servant with my Lord Mountjoy."[21]

Day's letter is written in Spanish and addressed to the "Señor Al-

mirante Mayor" (the Lord Grand Admiral). At the ti
two high dignitaries in Spain who sported such a t
Fadrique Enríquez, first cousin of King Fernando and C
of Castile. The other was Christopher Columbus. Altho
was usually called *almirante,* I have seen eleven documen
is given the title of *almirante mayor.* Two of these docume
signed by the King and Queen. If the Catholic Sovereigns
bus the title of Grand Admiral, there is no reason why
foreign merchant should not do the same.

As for the other Grand Admiral, Fadrique Enríquez, he
ited his title from his father. He was a landlubber, much mc
on a battlefield than on the deck of a ship, and he never sh
interest in voyages of discovery. Besides, at the time John Day
letter (winter 1497–1498), Fadrique seems to have been out
on a secret mission to Naples, where he was supposed to sta
column to pave the way for the conquest of the country
Spaniards.

In addition, there are other reasons for believing that Day
was addressed to Columbus. At the beginning, he mentions tw
which are known to have influenced the Genoese. The first is c
Inventio Fortunata. Day thought that he was bringing it with
Spain; but he could not find it in his baggage, and he apologiz
not sending it to Columbus. The author, Nicholas of Lynn, w
English monk who lived in the fourteenth century and claim
have traveled as far as the North Pole. Most historians believe tha
English friar's travels are imaginary; but some do admit that he
have ventured as far as Greenland.

In his letter John Day also mentions sending a copy of *Marco Po
Travels* to the Grand Admiral. Now, in the Biblioteca Colombiana
Seville, which was founded by Fernando Columbus, Christophe
younger son, there is an abridged Latin version of *Marco Polo's Trav*
that was probably printed in Antwerp in 1485. It was listed by Fe
nando as No. 2741 in the catalogue of his library. Fernando was i
the habit of noting down the price and date of acquisition of his books
since he did not do so for No. 2741, we can take it for granted that
he inherited it from his father. The book contains 366 marginal notes,
many of which were written in by Columbus. Could it be the copy
that Day sent to the "Lord Grand Admiral"?

Evidently Columbus was keenly interested in Cabot's discovery, for Day's letter was an answer to a request for *additional* information. The English merchant also sent a map, now lost, or rather a rough sketch he had made, showing the "capes and islands of the said land." This may be the sketch La Cosa used as a model for the outline of the "coast discovered by Englishmen" that is featured on his famous world map. Day's letter also contains details not found elsewhere. For example, he mentions that Cabot had noticed the magnetic variation of the needle; and he alludes to an alleged prediscovery. Of course there is no reason why the Admiral should not have learned of it during one of his trips to Bristol as a seafaring merchant.[22]

We shall say no more about this Bristol prediscovery, because it might lead us very far from the object of this study. We shall only point out that the most important feature of Day's letter, for Columbus in 1498, was the mention that a landmass had been found in the north, between 52°N. and 45°N., and that this landmass was considered part of the Grand Khan's empire. As he started on his third voyage, Columbus was anxious to redeem himself and to prove his detractors false. He could restore his waning prestige by discovering a real *tierra firme,* not just islands, and by bringing back real gold, not just *guanines,* alloys of low value. Moreover, he had been informed by the jeweler and amateur astronomer Jaime Ferrer that, if he wanted to strike it rich, he should go south, for only equatorial countries produced great amounts of gold, pearls, and spices.[23] As his goal he set the Golden Chersonese, an imaginary peninsula jutting out of the Gulf of Bengal, pictured in Ptolemy's *Geographia,* famous for its gold and its precious stones.

Columbus' Third Voyage

These are the reasons that prompted the Admiral to search for new land during his third voyage; but he kept his project secret until the last moment, a wise thing to do since he was not sure of success. There was an unfortunate result, however: before leaving Seville, Antón

Mariño's supplies had been loaded not only on the three vessels that were sent directly to Hispaniola, but also on two of the other three that went with Columbus on his detour. This delay and adverse weather conditions caused most of the food to spoil before reaching Santo Domingo.

The two squadrons took leave of each other in the vicinity of Gomera Island on 21 June, and Columbus, with his three ships, headed toward the Cabo Verde archipelago. In Santiago he obtained fresh meat, and he and his men visited a small island where lepers from Europe came to eat the flesh of the turtles and bathe in their blood, since this was considered the only cure for leprosy. After a week in Cabo Verde, the three vessels sailed southwest. Then on 13 July, the wind died down and the seas were becalmed. The heat was so intense that it looked as if the three ships would burst into flames, and in the holds the food supplies suffered great damage. After a week it rained and the wind returned. The fleet sailed again in a general southwest direction for about 17 days, to a latitude of 9°N., and then turned westward. Columbus thought that he would find things of value on that parallel, because it was the latitude of Guinea, whence came the Portuguese gold. On 31 July, an island was sighted that Columbus baptized *Trinidad*. As they came close, they saw a cape that looked like a galley, so they named it *Cabo de la Galera*. They were at the southeast corner of the island. The next few days they explored the south shore, then reached the western end of that coast, which they called *Punta del Arenal,* entered a passage between this point and the mainland, and cleared it with great difficulty because of the swiftness of the current. They baptized it *Boca de la Sierpe*. Then they found themselves in a placid gulf whose waters were as fresh as an island lake; but they could not understand why. They called it *Golfo de la Ballena.*

At first the Indians seemed to be afraid of them, but soon friendly relations were established. The natives went naked, except for a kerchief of woven cotton and dyed in various colors, which they wore over the head, and another, which they fastened around their loins in place of drawers. The climate was unusually mild in spite of the latitude, and mornings were chilly. They saw a great quantity of fish and oysters and many parrots.

Toward the northeast, at a distance of about 15 leagues from the

Punta del Arenal, Columbus saw a mountainous headland, which he mistook for an island and called *Islo de Gracia*. In reality, it was the eastern end of the Paria peninsula, where a long and steep cordillera stretches from east to west parallel to the shore. On 4 August, cutting across the Gulf of the Ballena, he sailed toward the cape he had seen and called *Cabo de Lapa*. Facing it, and separated from it by a narrow strait, he saw the northeast end of Trinidad, which he named *Cabo Boto*. Thinking, as we have already said, that Paria was an island, Columbus decided to cruise along its south shore, west from Cabo de Lapa, hoping to reach a passage that would lead him to the ocean. He found harbors and rivers, many strange tropical fruits and countless monkeys. The water was fresh, but not quite as sweet as lake water, for it had a slightly brackish taste that reminded him of the Guadalquivir. He was amazed at the mangrove trees whose roots stemmed from the sea; below the water level, innumerable oysters clung to these roots. Trying to determine how pearls are produced, the Genoese remembered Pliny's explanation, that they are formed by the dew that falls into oysters when they are open; and he admitted that this may well be true, because of the heavy dew on the shores of Paria. The innermost part of the Gulf of the Ballena he called the *Golfo de las Perlas*.

He had not yet found a passage between the Gulf of the Ballena and the ocean, and the sea bottom was becoming dangerously shallow. He dispatched the smallest of his three ships westward, toward what appeared to be an island. It turned out to be the north section of the Orinoco delta, which through its four branches poured out an unbelievable amount of fresh water into the Gulf of the Ballena. Columbus understood then why the waters of the gulf were so fresh. He also realized that such a huge river could not spring from an island but must come from a continent, and he changed the name of *Isla de Gracia* to *Tierra de Paria*. He had found what he had been looking for, and he decided not to tarry any more, but reach Santo Domingo as soon as possible, because, if there was further delay, the supplies he carried in his ships would become a total loss.[24]

He set his course for the strait he had noticed before between Cabo de Lapa and Cabo Boto; it was a most difficult passage to negotiate, for, in addition to two islets that stood in the middle (*Caracol* and *Delfin*), the fresh water current rushing out northward was met head on by the tide. Luckily, on that day the fresh water current was much the stronger, and it carried the three ships out of the channel into the open sea (12 August). Feeling as if he had escaped from a dragon's mouth, Columbus baptized the strait *Boca del Dragón*. To the north, he saw two islands, he called the first *Asunción* and the second *Concepción*. He set sail toward the west at some distance from the coast of the Paria peninsula, probably to avoid running into shoals, and because he was in a hurry to reach Santo Domingo. Then, on 15 August, he sighted an island whose twin mountain masses must have been visible to him for miles. He sailed toward it but did not land, passing between it and some rocky islets he called the *Frailes* (monks). He named the island *Margarita*, in honor of the widowed princess Margaret of Burgundy, whose wedding he had attended fifteen months before. It was unfortunate for the Genoese that he made no landings on the shores of Paria and in Margarita, for he could have amassed there a stock of pearls sufficient to appease most of the criticism leveled against him, and to make him regain the full confidence of his Sovereigns. The small quantity he had acquired in the Golfo de la Ballena was not enough to silence his enemies.

Following a northwest course, they sighted land on 19 August, and on the following day they cast anchor between Beata and Alta Vela, two small islands on the south coast of Hispaniola, 100 miles from Santo Domingo. He sent the boats to the mainland, to contact Indians and send a message to his brother Bartholomew who had been governing in his absence. Six of the natives came to the anchorage and climbed on board the *capitana* (flagship). One of them was carrying a fully equipped crossbow, a sign of ill omen. "Could it be that of a dead Spaniard?" For Indians were strictly forbidden to use or just possess European weapons, and it was a crime to give or sell them such arms. On the next day Bartholomew arrived. The two brothers greeted each other warmly, for they had not seen each other for almost two years and a half. Nevertheless, there was some anxiety, for Bartholomew brought news of Francisco Roldán's rebellion. Because of contrary winds, they did not reach Santo Domingo—which had replaced Isabela as the island's capital—until 31 August 1498.[25]

The "Earthly Paradise"

Two years earlier, before leaving for Spain, Columbus had put his brother Bartholomew in charge of the government of Hispaniola. During his absence, both the Indians and the settlers became very restive, the former because of an onerous gold tribute imposed upon them; the latter because their hopes of enriching themselves quickly had proved false, because the stipend they had been promised by the Crown had not been paid to them for months, and because they resented being ruled too strictly by a foreigner, not a Spaniard. They were tired of state control, they wanted to be in business for themselves, own large tracts of land, and use Indian labor. The leader of the malcontents was the *alcalde mayor* (chief justice) Francisco Roldán, who had taken control of Xaragua, the southwest portion of the island.

Some three weeks before Columbus arrived at Santo Domingo, the three ships he had dispatched directly from the Canaries reached Hispaniola, bringing immigrants and supplies; but their pilots missed the newly created harbor at the mouth of the Ocama, overshot their mark, and anchored on the coast of Xaragua, where Roldán held sway with his followers. The ships' captains, ignorant of the rebellion, let the *alcalde* come on board, entertained him, and allowed their men to land. Among them were criminals, who had volunteered to serve in Hispaniola because they had been promised a pardon; others were vagrants, enemies of work, law, and order. When Roldán showed his true colors, he had no trouble persuading them to take his side. Did he also manage to get hold of the supplies and food stored in the three vessels? Very likely, Antón Mariño had to hand over part of it to him. Thus reinforced, Roldán was able to hold both Christopher and Bartholomew in check. The Admiral, abandoned by most of the settlers, unable to use force, resorted to negotiation. Not until one year later was an agreement reached, Columbus acceding to most of the *alcalde*'s demands.[26]

Meanwhile, the five ships that had brought the men and supplies and were under contract to go back to Spain were being readied for their return trip. They were packed with Indian slaves, 600 according to Las Casas. Many of them died on board for lack of food, lack of air, or just lack of freedom. The armada sailed from Santo Domingo on 18 October, under the command of Giovanni Antonio, Columbus' cousin and mayordomo. To him the Admiral entrusted several letters for the Sovereigns.[27] In some he defended his conduct, recriminated against the rebels, and asked that someone be sent to administer justice. In another letter, he gave an account of his discovery of a vast expanse of *tierra firme*, to the south, near the equator. This new land, according to him, was another portion of Asia, the one that contained the Earthly Paradise.

Several arguments had led him to this conclusion, which may seem strange to us; but to many of his contemporaries it looked perfectly natural. We shall now discuss his arguments one by one.

1. During his crossing from the Canaries to Trinidad, he had noticed, through some miscalculation with his quadrant, that the North Star described larger circles around the pole than he had noted on his previous voyages, and these circles increased as he sailed southwest. When he reached Trinidad, he also remarked that the weather there was mild, more temperate than torrid, although he was near the equator. He concluded that the greater variation of the North Star and the mildness of the climate were due to the fact that the region he had reached had a greater altitude and was closer to Heaven. He explained this by asserting that the western hemisphere—which englobed the West Indies—was not perfectly round, but had some kind of elevation or mountain shaped like a woman's nipple. According to most theologians, a temperate climate in a torrid zone was one of the characteristics of the Earthly Paradise.[28]

2. In the *Golfo de las Perlas*, he had also noticed the amazing outflow of a fresh water current, which came from four arms of a huge river. It poured into the sea a tremendous amount of water, which retained its freshness for miles from the coast. Such an enormous stream must have its source in Paradise, for anyone who has read the Bible knows that Paradise is the source of four of the greatest rivers in the world (Nile, Ganges, Tigris, Euphrates).

3. Those who have read the Bible also know that "the Good Lord planted a garden in Eden in the East," and practically every medieval theologian worth his salt agreed that this *Hortus Deliciarum* (Garden of Delight), as poets called it, was located in East Asia, at the extreme end of the world. To some critics who objected that travelers had been

unable to find it, the Fathers of the Church explained that it was on top of a mountain so high that even the Deluge had failed to reach it, or that it was surrounded by walls of fire, or that it was separated from the rest of Asia by an arm of the ocean. Columbus also added that the luxuriant tropical forest, the fragrance of the foliage, the exotic birds with their multi-colored plumage and melodious songs, the savory fruit and odiferous spices that had delighted him in Paria were all characteristics of the Earthly Paradise.

The Mexican historian Edmundo O'Gorman has seen a contradiction in the fact that Columbus referred to the landmass he had discovered in the south as a *continent* or as a *new world,* asserting at the same time that it was where the earthly paradise could be found.[29] I see no contradiction. In the first place, O'Gorman uses the words *continent* and *world* in their modern sense, very different from the meaning they had in 1498. This has been ably demonstrated by Wilcomb Washburn.[30] In the Middle Ages, *continent* expressed continuity and contiguity. Isidore of Seville defined it as *perpetua terra nec ullo mari discreta* (continuous land not divided by any sea). The Spanish equivalent was *tierra firme,* and Columbus used it to mean "mainland" in opposition to "island." When he wrote that he had found a *tierra firme,* he meant a vast expanse of land, not a fourth part of the globe to be added to Europe, Asia, and Africa. When he used the term *otro mundo* (another world), he did so to convey the idea of a new landmass. He could say like Saint Clement: "The ocean—and the worlds beyond it . . . ."

This new mainland that Columbus had discovered he could well think was a portion of Asia, since the Earthly Paradise was so considered by many. For example, on the 1436 world map of Andrea Bianco, the Earthly Paradise occupies the end of a peninsula in the easternmost section of the Asiatic mainland. It is neatly outlined, and in it are pictured Adam, Eve, the Tree of Life, the Serpent, and the four rivers that flow out of it.[31] Two world maps printed from wood blocks in 1500 also show that Earthly Paradise and the four rivers in East Asia. Pierre d'Ailly, an author Columbus read carefully, also put the Earthly Paradise in the east, just below the equator on a mountain top: "ibi versus orientem in uno monte est paradisus terrestris." Columbus expressed his agreement, adding in the margin the following comment: "Paradisus terrestris ibi est."[32]

The Genoese concluded his letter to the Sovereigns with a remark directed at his critics, who had complained about the expense involved in his enterprise, and about the lack of short range profits. "They speak this without considering the shortness of the time, and how many difficulties there are to contend with, and that every year there are individuals who singly earn by their deserts out of Your Majesties' own household more revenue than would ever cover the whole of this expense." Quite true, but this judgment must have angered and disposed against him men of high rank who occupied influential positions at the Court.

With the letter, the Genoese sent a map picturing the newly found land, and 160 or 170 pearls (the sources do not agree as to the exact number). The letters, the map, and the pearls left Santo Domingo on 18 october, on which day the five vessels sailed under the command of Juan Antonio Colombo. Among those who went back to Europe with these five ships were Antón Mariño, and Las Casas' father. They reached Spain on 10 December 1498. In Seville, Antón Mariño must have reported to Fonseca and rendered an account to him. He must also have made some comments on the sad state of affairs in Hispaniola, and whatever he said did not fall on a deaf ear, since Fonseca had no love for Columbus.

The news must have also quickly reached the Court, then residing in Alcalá de Henares. Most likely, it was Juan Antonio who delivered the letters to the Sovereigns. The latter were doubtless pleased with the discovery and the pearls; but Columbus' prophetic tone, his conviction of the almost divine character of his mission, his lamentations and recriminations against Roldán and the settlers of Hispaniola must have produced a painful impression. Columbus wanted to send Bartholomew to Paria, to continue exploring the newly discovered land, but both brothers had their hands full with the Roldán rebellion. The time was ripe for others to take up the task of exploration, all the more so if it did not cost the Crown anything. Already in 1495, when it was rumored that the Admiral was dead, permission had been given to would-be discoverers; but after Columbus was heard from and protested that his privileges were being infringed, the authorization had been canceled. At the beginning of 1499, as the Sovereigns were thinking of removing the Genoese from the governorship of Hispaniola, they no longer had such scruples. They were ready to grant licenses for discovery to any qualified person willing to proceed at his own cost. It so happened that three men qualified for that task were at the Court at the time. The first was Alonso de Hojeda, a soldier who had distinguished himself in fighting the Indians of Hispaniola. The other two, Juan de la Cosa and Peralonso Niño, were experienced pilots who had accompanied Columbus on his first and second voyages. All three were shown the Admiral's letter and the map, and all three were granted permission to explore the coast of the new *tierra firme*. Two expeditions were organized. Hojeda and La Cosa were in charge of the first, which Amerigo Vespucci joined. Peralonso Niño undertook the other.

Naturally, this was in violation of the privileges granted to Columbus; but a bit of pre-Jesuit casuistry satisfied easily appeased consciences, like that of King Fernando, one of the shrewdest and most unscrupulous men of his time. The government alleged that when the Almirante discovered Paria, he did not land and take possession of it personally, but remained on his ship because he was ailing; therefore, he could make no claims to the new *tierra firme*. This was hotly denied by his partisans and those of his son Diego, and it became one of the main points of contention in the *Pleitos,* a series of lawsuits between the Crown and the Columbus family that went on for twenty-five years, and ended in compromise in 1536, when the descendants of the Genoese gave up their privileges in exchange for an annual pension and the title of Duke of Veragua, which they still use.[33]

2   The Business of Discovery

The Capitulation

The discovery of Paria by Columbus triggered a series of voyages whose aim was to further explore the newly found land, take possession of it in the name of Spain, and search for gold, pearls and precious stones. We know that at least eleven such voyages took place, in approximately the following chronological order.

	Principals	Departure	Return
1.	Alonso de Hojeda, Juan de la Cosa, and Amerigo Vespucci	18 May 1499	June 1500
2.	Peralonso Niño and Cristóbal Guerra	Early June 1499	c. 8 April 1500
3.	Vincente Yañez Pinzón	c. 1 December 1499	30 September 1500
4.	Diego de Lepe	Mid-December 1499	End of July 1500
5.	Alonso Vélez de Mendoza and Luis Guerra	After 18 August 1500	Before 9 June 1501
6.	Cristóbal Guerra and Diego Rodriguez de Grajeda	Late summer 1500	Before 1 November 1501
7.	Rodrigo de Bastidas and Juan de la Cosa	After 18 February 1501	September 1502
8.	Alonso de Hojeda, Juan de Vergara, and Garcia de Campos	January 1502	Summer 1503
9.	Cristóbal and Luis Guerra	Between 17 May and 18 July 1504	Did not return (died)
10.	Juan de la Cosa and Juan de Ledesma	Shortly after 18 September 1504	Before 13 March 1506
11.	Alonso de Hojeda and Pedro de la Cueva	After 6 June 1505	Did not return (settled in Hispaniola)

The organization of a voyage of discovery was no easy matter. First of all, an official authorization had to be secured. The Catholic Sovereigns had to be approached, and a plan had to be submitted to them. If the candidate could convince them that he was qualified for the job, and if they accepted his project, the King and Queen would refer the matter to Bishop Fonseca, who was in charge of the affairs of the Indies in Seville. We have two letters from Fernando and Isabel to Fonseca, ordering him to reach an agreement with Alonso de Hojeda and with Diego de Lepe respectively. Here is a rough translation of the beginning of the first letter: "Reverend Father Bishop of Cordoba. Hojeda submitted to us some articles which are included with this [letter] and which seem all right to us; and because we have been told that he is dependable and has served us well in matters relating to the Indies, as a service to us work out the terms of a contract in all the things that will seem most profitable to us, receiving from him any security you will deem proper. In consequence, We entrust and order you to attend to it without delay, and send us the articles and the act in the form that will seem most appropriate, signed and sealed by you, that We may decide for the best after We have seen what you advise."[1]

The second letter runs as follows: "Reverend Father Bishop of Cordoba . . . Diego de Lepe . . . has informed us that . . . he wishes to serve us again and make another voyage of discovery with three caravels to the region where he went before . . . and he begged us to grant him our authorization. . . . Therefore We ask you and entrust you to give him a license to discover with the said three caravels, under the conditions and in the manner habitual in such cases, and We give you full power to do so."[2]

Negotiating with Fonseca to obtain a license might be a matter of a few weeks, or it might drag on for months. In the case of Hojeda and Lepe, it took ten months; but Vélez de Mendoza waited only four or five weeks. The bishop would not give his consent until he felt sure that the applicant could finance his expedition. Once Fonseca became satisfied that enough money would be raised to outfit the ships, pay the crews and purchase the supplies, he was willing to discuss the terms of a contract. This contract was known in Spanish as an *asiento* or a *capitulación*.

We do not have all the capitulations that were granted, for some have been lost. Those for the Hojeda—La Cosa, Niño—Guerra, and Diego de Lepe voyages are missing. Since the Guerra—Grajeda expedition was a state enterprise, its leaders being in the service of the Crown, no capitulation was called for. In the case of the other seven voyages, the capitulations have been preserved, the oldest being the one made out to Vicente Yañez Pinzón on 6 June 1499. In addition, we have the *asientos* for four projected expeditions that did not materialize. They were granted to Yañez Pinzón (5 September 1501), Diego de Lepe (14 September 1501), Juan de Escalante (5 October 1501), and Rodrigo de Bastidas (14 February 1504).[3]

Usually, but not always, the first clause of the capitulation specified the number of vessels the applicant would be allowed to sail with. The number varied from two to ten, but it was at best tentative, for it was fairly easy to obtain later an increase or decrease according to circumstances.

Then the capitulation stated explicitly the territories that the expedition *could not* explore. In the earliest *asientos* (for example, in the one granted to Yañez Pinzón on 6 June 1499), the only restrictions applied to the lands discovered by Columbus (the West Indies), and to those assigned to Portugal by the Treaty of Tordesillas in 1494, that is, the lands east of the partition line. But when those early expeditions returned to Spain, their leaders laid exclusive claims to the territories they had discovered; therefore, new restrictions had to be added in the capitulations that were made up afterward. For example, Niño and Guerra came back in April 1500, claiming that they had discovered a coast rich in pearls, the *Costa de las Perlas* (central Venezuela); so when Vélez de Mendoza and Rodrigo de Bastidas applied for *asientos* the following month, the *Costa de las Perlas* was declared out of bounds for them. Then, in June Hojeda returned, laying claims to a land called *Arquibacoa* or *Coquibacoa* (Maracaibo region), where he said he had found green stones (emeralds?); and in July Vélez was made to swear, in a revised version of his capitulation, that he would keep out of Coquibacoa in addition to the Costa de las Perlas.[4]

One year later, in June 1501, Hojeda was granted a license to go back to Coquibacoa, the land he had discovered two years earlier; but he was denied access to the Costa de las Perlas, whose limits were set in his capitulation. He was strictly forbidden to land there on his way to Coquibacoa, and the royal *veedores* (comptrollers) on his ships were ordered to make sure that he did not violate that prohibition.[5]

Later, as more expeditions returned to Spain, and as claims were laid to further discoveries, the wording of the capitulation was changed. The new applicants were refused access to "any land already discovered," in addition to those found by Columbus or belonging to

Portugal. Then, after Yañez Pinzón and Lepe had explored from Cape Santo Agostinho to Paria, and after Bastidas and La Cosa had sailed westward from Coquibacoa to Central America, no more land was left to be discovered. As a result, interest in discovery began to lag. To revive it, all restrictions were lifted, all the lands were thrown open, except those discovered by Columbus or assigned to Portugal that still remained taboo. The claims to special sections of the coast and the governorships were abolished. Only Coquibacoa was still set aside for Hojeda, because he was supposed to settle fifty soldiers and build a fort there, according to the terms of the capitulation he received in September 1504; but this plan for a permanent settlement failed or was not carried out, for Hojeda did not stay in Coquibacoa but moved to Hispaniola.

In his *asiento,* the leader of each expedition was also granted all the rights that went with the title of *capitán general* (commander-in-chief). His orders had to be obeyed, he had complete jurisdiction "civil and criminal," and he could punish all offenders. He could not, however, sentence to death or to loss of limb. Such penalties could be inflicted only by the Crown.

Most of the capitulations had no political implications. They were mainly authorizations for exploration and commercial intercourse with the natives. Of course, the *capitán general* was expected to earmark the coast and take possession of it in the name of Spain; but this did not involve permanent occupation, settling the land, building towns or fortified outposts. The two *asientos* granted to Hojeda in 1501 and 1504 are different, however, for they show political and military considerations. In 1501, Fernando and Isabel were afraid that the English might be coming down from the north in search of a passage to India. To stop them, Hojeda was ordered in his capitulation to place along the shore, at frequent intervals, markers of stone or wood on which the arms of Castile were to be carved. The 1504 capitulation went much further. It provided for the building of a fort to be garrisoned by fifty soldiers under Hojeda's command; but as we have already stated, nothing came out of this project for the military occupation of Coquibacoa.

The King's Share

Naturally, in exchange for granting a capitulation, the government expected something in return, that is, a share of the profits. This share varied from one fourth to one sixth, and was not always agreed upon without arduous negotiations, as was the case with La Cosa in 1503–1504. Here is a schema of the King's share, as it varied in the different *asientos* that have come down to us:

Yañez Pinzón (1499)		*quinto* (fifth) of the net
Vélez de Mendoza (1500)		*cuarto* (fourth) of the net
Bastidas (1500)		*cuarto* of the net
Hojeda (1501)		*quinto* of the net
Yañez Pinzón (1501)		*quinto* of the net
Lepe (1501)	Old land	*mitad* (half) of the net
	New land	*sexto* (sixth) of the net
Escalante (1501)		*sexto* (not specified whether net or gross)
C. Guerra (1504)		*quinto limpio* (free fifth) of the gross
La Cosa (1504)		*quinto limpio* of the gross
Bastidas (1504)		*quinto limpio* of the gross
Hojeda (1505)	Old land	*quinto limpio* of the gross
	New land	*sexto* (not specified whether net or gross)

Vélez and Bastidas seem to have been less favored than the others, since they were required to pay one fourth of the net, but this is only apparent, for one fourth of the net was considered equivalent to one fifth of the gross; therefore, it does not seem that these two fared worse than Cristóbal Guerra and La Cosa did four years later. In the case of Lepe (1501) and Hojeda (1504), who had already been in South America, it should be noted that they were granted more favorable terms for booty acquired in lands still to be discovered (one sixth), than in territories they had already explored (one half for Lepe, one fifth of the gross for Hojeda). No doubt this was meant as an incentive for further discovery. Also, when on the same day capitulations were awarded to two or more applicants, the Crown played no favorite, but granted equal terms. On 5 June 1500, Vélez and Bastidas received identical *asientos*, and the same thing happened in 1504 to Cristóbal Guerra, La Cosa, and Bastidas. Because the *quinto* was usually the percentage of the King's share, a new word was coined in the Spanish language, the verb *quintar*, which meant to pay the Crown its due.

The profits from which the King's share was to be deducted were expected to come from products having a high commercial value. In the earlier capitulations (Yañez Pinzón, 1499; Vélez and Bastidas, 1500), these prized commodities are enumerated as follows: "gold, silver, copper, tin, mercury, pearls, precious stones, jewels, black or mulatto slaves . . . monsters, serpents and any other animals, fish or birds, spices and drugs, and other things of value."[6]

Slaves were included in the list, that is, African slaves, Negroes and mulattoes. No mention was made of Indian slaves, because the Queen probably thought they were implicitly excluded. But Hojeda and Vespucci brought back, in June 1500, 200 Indian captives who were sold publicly.[7] Yañez Pinzón brought back more, and so did Diego de Lepe. The latter handed over his Indians to Fonseca, who, instead of freeing them, seems to have allowed them to be sold. He and his colleagues, Ximeno de Briviesca (in Cadiz) and Gonzalo Gómez de Cervantes (in Jerez), who helped him handle matters relating to the Andalusian voyages, appear to have been perfectly indifferent to Indian slavery. Gómez de Cervantes himself was a slave owner, and in 1488, by order of the Crown, he had sold at public auction in Seville a large number of Moors captured in Malaga.[8] The Queen soon reacted to the indifference of her public servants, and in the capitulations granted in 1501 to Hojeda, Yañez Pinzón, Lepe and Escalante, the authorization relating to Negro and mulatto slaves was left out and replaced with the interdiction to bring any slaves at all. Isabel did not object, however, when Vélez de Mendoza and Luis Guerra sold their Indian captives in the summer or fall of 1501, and she even collected her share on these sales. Such tolerance may have been prompted by the fact that the natives brought back by Vélez and Luis Guerra came from a land called *Topia* (Brazil), and were subjects of Portugal, not of Castile. But when Cristóbal Guerra, in November 1501, began selling in various cities of Andalusia a large number of Indians he had captured on Bonaire Island, Isabel became very indignant, ordered his arrest, and had the wretched natives set free, because, as she put it herself, they were "subditos de nuestros reinos" (subjects of our kingdoms).[9]

Yet her displeasure with Cristóbal did not last very long. Her own views on Indian slavery were beginning to be mollified, and less than two years later she accepted the principle that "cannibals" or rebellious Indians such as the natives of Cartagena Bay and the Gulf of Urabá, could be sold as slaves. In October 1503, she signed an edict legalizing slave hunting in those regions,[10] and in the capitulations granted to Cristóbal Guerra, La Cosa, and Bastidas four months later (14 February 1504), a clause was introduced allowing them to bring back slaves from the Bay of Cartagena and adjacent islands.

As for exotic animals, birds, and reptiles, we know that many monkeys and parrots were obtained from the natives. Probably some iguanas and snakes were also captured and taken on board; but few if any must have survived the trip. We only know of one "monster" that reached Spain alive: a female opossum captured with her litter by Yañez Pinzón's men on the Isla de la Raposa (Trinidad?) in the spring of 1500. Her young died one by one during the crossing. Unable to accustom herself to a new climate and new surroundings, the mother passed out of existence a few weeks after landing. She was carefully examined by Pietro Martire and some of his learned friends. They marveled at her, for they had never seen a marsupial before, an animal who carries her young in an abdominal pouch like the kangaroo. Opossums are the only marsupials native to America.[11]

Brazilwood was not included among the things of value that could be brought back in the Andalusian voyages, probably because the Crown wanted to keep it a state monopoly. Most capitulations make no mention of it; those that do limit the quantity that can be introduced in Spain to very small amounts (not more than two quintals for Lepe in 1501, not more than a quintal for Escalante), or they even prohibit any quantity. Vicente Yañez Pinzón was told in 1499: "You cannot bring any brazil whatsoever, because it is the will of their Highnesses." Yet he returned to Spain with 350 quintals, which he was allowed to sell because he had brought back nothing else of value, and the sale of this brazilwood was the only way he could pay his debts and satisfy his creditors.[12] Hojeda, Cristóbal Guerra, Bastidas also cut and brought back brazilwood. With this, and with the amounts imported by the Crown from its preserve in Santo Domingo, near *Puerto Brazil* (Jacmel) in Xaragua province, the market became saturated and the price fell. In 1504, new outlets had to be found by the officials of the *Casa de la Contratación* (House of Trade) for the brazilwood brought back by Bastidas. Attempts were made to sell it in Genoa and in Flanders, where it was thought it might fetch a better price.[13]

To avoid any cheating that might deprive the Crown from part of its share, all the capitulations prescribed that on each vessel there should be an official called *escrivano* (secretary or clerk), or *veedor* (comptroller). This official was a representative of the government. Until the House of Trade was founded in 1503, Gonzalo Gómez de Cervantes, uncle of Bishop Fonseca and *corregidor* of Jerez, appointed such officials by order of the Queen. The duties of the *escrivano* or *veedor* were twofold: he had to keep record of anything of value (gold, silver, pearls, precious stones) acquired during the voyage, and he had to watch over it until the return home, keeping it safely locked in an *arca de dos llaves,* a trunk or safe with two different keys, the *escrivano* holding one, and the other being kept by the captain or the master of the vessel.

On the homeward journey, stopovers were forbidden, except in case of *force majeure* (stormy weather, lack of food or water). The ships were to make port at Seville or Cadiz, and there the captains were to render account to the official in charge (Briviesca in Cadiz, Fonseca in Seville) and hand over to him the King's *quinto.*

To protect the investors from such frauds as padding the ships' rolls and list of supplies by unscrupulous captains or masters, there was a provision for a thorough inspection of the fleet shortly before it sailed. Then the muster roll was carefully checked, and so was the cargo of food, supplies, and merchandise. In 1504 Cristóbal Guerra's armada left Seville before submitting to this control, and Ludovico Pinelo, factor of the House of Trade, was dispatched to Sanlucar de Barrameda, at the mouth of the Guadalquivir, where the inspection took place. Since this involved additional expense, and since the blame was put on Cristóbal, the latter had to foot the bill.[14] To avoid any similar occurrence, the clause was modified in the next capitulation (Hojeda's, 30 September 1504). It specified that should the armada leave Seville unexpectedly, and should the inspection have to take place in Sanlucar or Cadiz or some other port, the *capitán general* would be held responsible and would have to pay for the additional expense.

Finally, as a guarantee that he would comply with all the clauses in the capitulation, the *capitán general* had to give sureties and post bonds before sailing. He usually chose his bondsmen among wealthy and influential friends, men who could take up his defense before the Crown and other possible accusers when he returned from his voyage. In November 1504, Hojeda picked as one of his bondsmen a distinguished naval commander, Charles de Valera, son of the chronicler and royal adviser Mosen Diego de Valera.[15] Like Hojeda, the Valeras were from Cuenca. They were *conversos* and descended from the famous Jewish doctor Chirino, author of medical treatises and private physician to King Juan II of Castile.

Financing the Voyage

Once the would-be discoverer had obtained his capitulation, he had to lease and outfit ships, hire crews, buy supplies, food, and merchandise. This he could not do alone, and he had to find associates willing to provide the needed capital. The relationship between the partners might be very loose, or it might take the form of a company of shareholders. Let us consider the first type, for example the Vélez de Mendoza–Luis Guerra partnership. It was the simplest of all, since each of the two associates provided his own vessel and outfitted it, hired his own crew and paid for his own expenses. Still, it meant a fair amount of capital; for an impoverished hidalgo like Vélez, it meant borrowing money.

Stringent rules governed the Spanish money market, for both Church and State forbade usury. Christ had said: "Lend without expecting anything in return"; therefore, lending for profit was unchristian and illegal. The *Siete Partidas* of King Alfonso the Wise (Alfonso X) ordered that if a usurer did not repent and make amends before his death, he should be refused religious burial.[16] Alfonso XI in 1348, and the Catholic Sovereigns in 1480, again forbade *usuria*.

There were some cases, however, in which interest might be charged because of the risk involved, when merchandise was shipped abroad or across the sea. If the vessel sank or was captured by pirates, or if the cargo was lost, the borrower was released from his obligation to reimburse the lender who would forfeit his investment; but if the venture was successful, the lender would be entitled to a profit.

In Roman law, the capital thus invested at a risk by the lender was called *nauticum foenus,* and the chance of loss that he incurred was known as *periculum pretii.* The Romans had not invented this type of commercial legislation; they had borrowed it from the Athenians. The Byzantine emperor Justinian later amended and tightened it. Since an exorbitant rate of interest was sometimes charged by the lender, Justinian limited it to 12 per cent.[17] This rate may still have been the legal one in Spain around the year 1500, but in the practice it was probably much higher. How high it was cannot be ascertained, since no interest rate was mentioned in writing to avoid possible trouble with the Church or with the authorities. Some thirty years later, the emperor Charles V, himself a heavy borrower, admitted that usury was a frequent practice, and he limited the interest to 10 per cent.[18]

The same legislation applied if, instead of borrowing money, the captain or master of a vessel bought merchandise or food on credit promising to pay for it on his return at the price prevailing then plus a fair profit; but this often created complications as Yañez Pinzón and Diego de Lepe found out. Both had received from Palos merchants stocks of merchandise, for which they were to pay with interest at the end of their voyage. Yañez was away ten months, and Lepe about eight. During their absence, prices went up, and when they returned, the merchants clamored for huge increases amounting to 80 per cent or more for the price of their commodities. Both navigators appealed to the Crown to get a fair deal from their creditors and the local authorities. We have several Spanish sixteenth century treatises on usury, composed by theologians, in which are exposed the dishonest practices of the vendors who sold merchandise on credit.[19]

We have already seen that if the undertaking proved a failure the borrower was not obligated to pay back his debt, but in case of success he was bound to settle it within a certain lapse of time. If he failed to do so before the date set, he incurred a heavy penalty which increased as time passed on, and which could reach—but not exceed—twice the amount of the loan. This penalty was known in Spanish as *la pena del doblo* (the penalty of the double). The Spaniards had inherited it from the Romans through Justinian. It is mentioned in many documents of the notarial archives in Seville.

For example, on 9 May 1500, Vélez de Mendoza took an option on a ship called the *San Pedro*. A lease of 9,000 maravedis a month was agreed on for the duration of the voyage, to be paid 20 days after its return to Seville "under the penalty of the double" (*so la pena del doblo*).[20] The deal fell through because one of the co-owners of the *San Pedro* had other plans, and Vélez sailed on another vessel. Yet we have here a fairly common type of transaction, for other models of it are recorded in the Archives of Seville.

There was another way of raising money for a voyage of discovery, and Vélez used it also. To outfit his vessel he needed supplies, and to buy supplies he borrowed 15,000 maravedis from Carlos de Hontiveros, but in the contract no mention was made and no date was set for the paying back of the sum. It was stated, however, that it should earn interest as was customary in the shipping trade (*que gane según usamos de armazón*). This meant that the 15,000 maravedis were not a loan but an investment. Carlos de Hontiveros became a stockholder entitled to a percentage of the profits. Vélez completed a similar transaction on 27 May, when he obtained an additional 10,000 maravedis from Pedro Maldonado. In the contract it was stipulated that the sum would earn as was customary in the shipping trade. If the expedition was a success, Maldonado could expect to receive a profit proportional to his capital. In these two transactions, Hontiveros and Maldonado were not lenders but investors. They became Vélez's partners in a company, sharing in his success or in his failure.[21]

Forming a *compañía* was a common way to finance a voyage of discovery. The company of investors originated in Italy. It flourished in Genoa, Venice, Pisa, Florence, where it was known as a *commenda* or as a *societas*. Both the Church and the secular authorities approved of it because of the risk involved. Since the investors were in danger of losing their capital in case of failure, it was felt that they were entitled to a dividend if the venture was a success. Thomas Aquinas himself had said so, and his words on the subject were often quoted by bankers and theologians.[22]

A company might consist of only two or three partners, or it might include dozens of them. Of the smaller type many examples are found. In 1496 a Triana mariner, Juan Rodríguez de la Mesquita, formed a partnership with a barber and a blacksmith. Mesquita was to provide the ship and the crew; the other two would load the vessel with goods which were to be sold in the Canaries. The profits were to be divided in the usual way: ⅓ for the ship, ⅓ for the crew, ⅓ for the merchandise.[23] In March 1501 another Triana mariner, Diego de Grajeda, formed a company with the Genoese merchant, Jacome de Riberol, for the joint ownership of a 140-ton caravel yet to be built, whose cost was estimated at 250,000 maravedis. Grajeda would build and outfit the ship, and Riberol would pay him 125,000 maravedis.[24]

Among the Andalusian voyages, we find a striking example of a *compañía* with a very limited membership. On 5 June 1501, Alonso de Hojeda, who needed backers for his second expedition to Coquibacoa, entered into an association (*compañía y hermandad*) with two wealthy merchants named Juan de Vergara and García de Campos. The text of their *concordia* (agreement) has been preserved. According to it, each of the three was to provide one third of the capital required for the financing of the expedition, and all three would share equally in the profits. The revenues of the land and even the salary Hojeda was to receive from the Crown as governor of Coquibacoa were to be divided equally among the three partners. In addition all three would share equally in the command of the expedition; all the decisions were to be reached unanimously or by majority vote.[25]

Of the larger type of *compañía*, we have three examples: the Bastidas expedition of 1501, the projected voyage of Diego de Lepe which was canceled (winter 1501–1502), and the La Cosa armada of 1504. In all three cases, the minutes of the stockholders' meeting, held a few days before the fleet was supposed to sail, have been preserved in the notarial archives of Seville. The most complete records are for the Bastidas voyage, for in addition to the list of investors (twenty of them) we also find the amount that each put up. The sums varied from 5,000 to 50,000 maravedis, and the total was 375,547 maravedis. In case of disaster the investors would gracefully accept the loss of their capital (unless there had been malpractice on the part of the *capitán general*); but should the expedition return safely to Seville, provisions were made for splitting the profits in the following manner. First, the King's share would be deducted, then a flat sum of

100,000 maravedis would be set aside for the investors. Finally, whatever was left of the surplus would be divided into three equal shares: one for the shipowners, the second for the crews, and the third for the investors. The three-way sharing of the profits was customary, but the prior deduction of 100,000 maravedis in favor of the investors was very unusual and I have found no other example of it. It did give the latter a decided advantage. The dividend paid to each was to be proportional to his investment, according to the formula *sueldo por libra* (penny per pound), which is found in many documents.[26]

In the case of Diego de Lepe's voyage that was canceled, the board meeting took place on 25 November 1501. Only eleven investors attended. Lepe acknowledged reception of the sums invested in the expedition (unfortunately no figures are given in the minutes). He also promised to keep complete records, to return directly to Cadiz or Seville, to render accounts, and not to unload until he was duly authorized. If he or his subordinates did not keep such pledges, each could be fined 1,000 gold *castellanos*.[27]

For his 1504 voyage to the Gulf of Urabá, Juan de la Cosa held a meeting of his backers on 11 September, a few days before sailing. Some forty investors attended, but a few of the signatures are mere scratches of the pen or marks made by people who could not write. Yet, thirty-three of the names can be deciphered. Three of the investors were women. One signed her own name; for the other two, their husbands signed. There is a reference to the *ventaja* (bonus) which La Cosa was to receive as *capitán general* and chief pilot. It was calculated at 2.5 per cent of the capital and estimated at 30,000 maravedis. Therefore, the sums invested in the expedition must have totaled 1,200,000 maravedis. The shipowners had freighted out their vessels at a fixed monthly rate, and had been paid out of the capital four months' advance rent. Hence, they were not entitled to any dividend, and the profits were to be split in the following manner: one third for the crews and two thirds for the investors.[28]

The temporary partnerships formed by Bastidas, Lepe, and La Cosa were the prelude to others, like the *compañía* formed by Magellan to help finance his voyage around the world; but the most famous was the one chartered at Panama on 10 March 1526 by Francisco Pizarro, Diego de Almagro and Fernando de Luque, whose aim was nothing less than the conquest of Peru. Other countries, too, had their companies. The Company of *Adventurers of the New Foundland Land* operating out of Bristol was chartered in 1500. Its members were Englishmen and Portuguese from the Azores.[29]

Ships and Crews

Once the would-be discoverer had secured financial backing for his voyage, he had to find ships and crews, and this was no easy matter, for there was a shortage of both due to the wars in Italy. In 1501, Bastidas solved the problem by freighting two vessels from Bilbao and hiring their crews. In Seville, a great part of the shipping available for the American trade was in the hands of the *comitres,* a closely knit *hermandad* (brotherhood) of mariners who lived in the Magdalena parish or across the river in Triana. A *comitre* was a sort of naval reserve officer who served with his own ship whenever he was called for duty. Organized in 1252 by Alfonso X, the *comitres* were originally in charge of the royal galleys that were built and kept in the *atarazanas* (arsenal) of Seville. Three of them sailed on each galley, the youngest being in command, the other two acting as advisers. For twenty-one galleys, there were sixty-three *comitres.* They enjoyed the same franchises as the nobles, were exempt from taxation, could carry arms, dress in silk, and wear gold and silver ornaments. They had their own chapel and hospital on the *Plaza de los Comitres* in the Magdalena parish, and their own court of law where they settled their disputes.[30] After 1480, however, the galleys fell into disuse and disappeared, being replaced by sailing vessels. The arsenal was empty, but the banks of the Guadalquivir were teeming with caravels and *naos* (cargo ships). Many of them belonged to the *comitres,* who navigated with them to the Canaries, England, Flanders, or the Indies. Although they no longer had galleys, the *comitres* still owed service to the Crown. They were a wealthy class, proud of its privileges, and since a deceased member was often replaced by a son, a brother, or a nephew, they had almost become a hereditary clan. We shall have occasion later in this study to deal with *comitres* whose names are connected with early voyages to the New World, such as Luis Rodríguez de la Mesquita (father of Juan already mentioned), the Tiscareño brothers, Diego Rodríguez de Grajeda (already mentioned), and the pilot Bartolomé Diaz.

Two different types of ships were used in the Andalusian voyages: the *nao* and the *caravel.* The *nao* (contraction for *navio*), like the carrack of northern countries, was a merchant vessel. It was rounder than the caravel, wider at the beam, its width being one half of keel length and one third of deck length. (This was the *rule of one, two, three*). The hold was larger and could store more food and heavy cargo; but because of its shape and heavier load, it was slower than the caravel. The biggest of Columbus' three ships on his first voyage, the *Santa María,* was a *nao.* The Bastidas—La Cosa armada of 1501 consisted of a caravel and a *nao.* At the meeting of the investors already mentioned, it was decided that if Bastidas wished to send back the *nao* with a cargo of merchandise and keep exploring with the caravel, he could do so. *Naos* had a crow's nest on top of the mainmast, from which pirate ships could be detected.

The *caravel* seems to have derived its name from the Greek, with some Arabic alterations. It was lighter and more slender than the nao, and it was faster. Its stern was less bulging; its beam was only three tenths of deck length. Its hold depth was also inferior. According to the *Libro Nautico* of the Lisbon National Library, its average proportions were supposed to be the following: beam to depth of hold 2.30, keel to beam 2.40, deck length to beam 3.33. On top of the main deck (*cubierta*) were two short decks; the one at the bow was the *tilla.* It was then a simple structure, but later turned into the forecastle. At the stern, there was an afterdeck called *tolda.* Under it the captain had his quarters.[31]

Martinez-Hidalgo gives in meters the dimensions of one of Columbus' caravels, *la Niña,* as follows: overall length 21.44, length of deck 20.10; keel 15.46, beam 6.44, depth of hold 2.80, draft 1.78, tonnage 52.72 tons.[32]

Some caravels reached larger proportions and considerable tonnage; but for voyages of discovery navigators preferred the smaller type, which had a lesser draw and could be used in shallow coastal waters. During his third voyage, while sailing along the coast of Paria, Columbus complained that his vessels were too big for a voyage of discovery, since one was over 100 tons, and the other two over 70, "and he had no wish to go for discoveries, except with smaller ones. Because the ship he had on his first voyage (the *Santa Maria*) was a large one, she was lost in the harbor of Navidad."[33] This was also the opinion of Cristóbal Guerra. In a 1503 letter to Don Alvaro de Portugal, he remarked that for exploration the most appropriate vessels were the small caravels not exceeding 50 tons.[34]

A ship's tonnage was calculated by the number of pipes of wine (hogsheads) it could carry. The Seville ton was equivalent to two pipes or eight cubic cubits (1.400 cubic meters or 49.4 cubic feet). There was in Bilbao a ton of larger size, the *tonel macho* (1.683 cubic meters), but it was scarcely used in Andalusia at the time of the discovery of America.[35]

At the end of the fifteenth century, caravels were usually equipped with two different types of sails. The Portuguese favored the square sails, which by a misnomer were also called *redondas* (round), while they really were rectangular. Because of its large canvas surface, the square sail was ideal for long voyages on the ocean and for taking advantage of the following winds. The Spaniards, used to navigation in the Mediterranean, with shorter distances and frequent changes of course, preferred the triangular or *lateen* sails, which made it possible to steer closer to the wind. At the turn of the century, for ocean sailing, it became customary to combine both styles of rig. Square sails were usually carried on the foremast and main, and lateen sails on the mizzen. At the start of his first voyage of discovery, in 1492, Columbus had the rig on the *Niña* changed: "From lateen they made her redonda."[36] This meant that they rigged the foremast and mainmast with square sails.

The rudder consisted of a long flat piece of timber nearly perpendicular, hanging outside the stern. It hinged on the sternpost by means of pintles. To it, at right angle, was fitted the tiller, a long horizontal wooden beam or pole that the helmsman maneuvered. The steering wheel did not come into use until the eighteenth century.

Each caravel and nao had two service boats. The larger one was the *bergantín* (shallop or launch). It had nothing in common with the modern brigantine. It was an open boat about eight meters long. It could be manned by oar, but carried one or two masts. It was used to load or unload the ship, and for exploration and navigation close to shore or upriver, in shallow waters where a bigger vessel could not venture. It was usually carried in tow by the mother ship.

The other embarcation was the *batel* (yawl or pinnace). It was about a third smaller than the bergantin, had between five and or six benches of oarsmen and an auxiliary sail. When the mother ship was anchored, the *batel* was used to maintain communications with the shore, relay messages, transport officers or visitors. At sea it was carried on the deck of the mother ship. Martinez-Hidalgo cites an old Spanish saying: *Batel dentro, amigos fuera* (Boat in, friends out).[37]

The Bastidas—La Cosa expedition took along a *chinchorro,* a fishing boat bigger than the batel, but smaller than the bergantin. It usually carried one sail.

Being a ship's captain on an Andalusian voyage did not require much knowledge of seamanship or navigation, for the title usually went to a relative or a business associate of the *capitán general.* In 1501 Hojeda appointed his nephew Pedro, and his two partners both merchants. In 1504 Cristébal Guerra named his nephew Alonso de Monroy. Two of La Cosa's captains in 1504 were Juan de Ledesma and Juan de Quecedo, both heavy investors. Vélez de Mendoza even promised command of a vessel to an innkeeper who had loaned him large sums.

The ship was really run by the pilot and the master, both experienced seamen. The pilot had either served with Columbus or had sailed on some previous voyage. As for the master, if he did not own the vessel himself, he usually had been in the service of the owner a long time.

Next to them ranked the *escrivano* or *veedor.* He was the representative of the Crown and kept a record of the loot. The *escrivanos* were at first appointed by Gonzalo Gómez de Cervantes. Later, the *Casa de la Contratación* (House of Trade), founded in 1503, chose them. In addition to the salary they received from the government, they were entitled to the pay of an able seaman.

Below them came the petty officers. There was a *contramaestre* (mate or boatswain) who handled the crew, and a *despensero* (steward) who distributed the food rations. There were also several *oficiales,* men who had an *oficio* (skilled trade). On each vessel served a cooper, a carpenter, and a caulker. A barber cured wounds and did minor surgery. Sometimes we also find a *fisico* (physician), and one or two *lombarderos* (artillerymen). The latter operated lombards (or bombards) of wrought iron, which were mounted on wooden carriages on the deck. These guns were loaded at the breech, and they fired stone cannon balls at a maximum range of 300 meters.

Among the members of the Hojeda expedition to Coquibacoa (1502–1503), were half a dozen *plateros* (gold or silversmiths) whose job was to locate gold mines and assay gold objects and precious stones. In this voyage also sailed an apothecary who collected herbs and medicinal plants.

As for the sailors, they were divided into three categories: the *marineros* (able seamen), the *grumetes* (apprentice seamen) and the *pajes* (cabin boys). We have the pay scale for the Guerra—Grajeda voyage of 1500–1501.[38]

Peralonso Niño and Vicente Yañez Pinzón hired quite a few relatives as *marineros,* who were probably professional seamen. Less experienced must have been the capitalists who enlisted as sailors and took part in a voyage to keep an eye on their investment. This was a fairly common practice, and we have several examples of it. When the Bastidas expedition returned to Seville in the fall of 1502, some investors collected pay for their *marinaje* (seamanship) in addition to the dividend on their investment.[39]

Not a single member of the clergy, secular or regular, seems to have taken part in any of the Andalusian voyages. When the Queen tentatively approved Cristóbal Guerra's 1503 project for a new expedition to America, she proposed that some monks be sent along to watch over the spiritual welfare of the crews and do some evangelizing among the Indians; but this suggestion was left out of the final draft capitulation granted to Guerra, La Cosa, and Bastidas. Probably it was felt that on such voyages there was neither time nor opportunity to preach the Gospel to the natives. Moreover, any attempt to restrain the behavior of the crews would have been most unwelcome.

As for women, we have no record of any of them being allowed to join such expeditions. This did not mean that the crews would be deprived of female companionship, for as soon as they reached the shores of America, they found Indian girls who accommodated them willingly or forcibly.

The muster roll of a fifty- to sixty-ton caravel averaged between 25 and 35. The men on Vespucci's two ships totaled 57, while the combined crews on Bastidas' caravel and nao added up to about 65, and the

Niño-Guerra vessel carried 33 persons. Naturally, larger ships had bigger crews. When plans were made in 1500 for the Guerra-Grajeda voyage, the one hundred-ton caravel was allotted 40 men, and the smaller fifty-ton vessel a crew of 30.

At first, most of Seville's seafaring activities were concentrated on the river bank fronting the Magdalena parish and the *Barrio de la Mar* (waterfront district); but as the increasing tonnage of the vessels required a deeper channel, and as wider spaces were needed for ship building, careening, and loading, the port of Seville began spreading downstream, an expansion that is still in progress today. Between the Triana bridge and the Torre del Oro, on the muddy banks of the Arenal, naos, caravels, and other sailing vessels replaced the defunct galleys of the royal navy that were no longer in use. And across the Guadalquivir, the Triana waterfront was expanding downstream from the Santa Ana church, teeming with artisans working in the shipyards, with mariners of all categories, and with shop and tavern keepers and their clientele, while the *cambiadores* (moneychangers) and the *corredores de lonja* (brokers) acted as intermediaries between the merchants and the ships, between the city and river. It is too early yet to speak of industrialization, but some local products were beginning to be manufactured on a fairly large scale. Such were pottery and ceramics, whose fabrication still flourishes in Triana. When Hieronymus Münzer was there in November 1494, he marveled at the huge size of the oil and wine jars made out of potter's clay; "If I had not seen it, I would not have believed it."[40] *Jarcia* (ship rigging) was also manufactured. And there were *hornos* (ovens) for the baking of hardtack. The flour used for this came from water mills, or from *atahonas* whose grinding stones were powered by mules. As for the making of soap, Seville had been holding the monopoly in Castile for over eighty years.

Moneys and Measures

In most official records, the monetary unit used was the *maravedi*. The name is of Arabic origin. According to Thacher, it was worth approxi-

WEIGHTS AND MEASURES IN CASTILE[41]

Lineal Measures

Marine league	4 Roman miles (3.18 nautical miles)
Land league	3 Roman miles (4,440 meters)
Roman mile	5,000 *pies* (1,480 meters, 1,620 yards)
Vara (yard)	2 *codos* or 3 *pies* (84 centimeters, 33 inches)
Codo (cubit)	(42 centimeters)
Pie (foot)	4 *palmos* or 12 *pulgadas* (28 centimeters, 11 inches)
Palmo (palm)	3 *pulgadas* (7 centimeters, 3 inches)
Pugada (inch)	

Arid Measures

Cahiz	12 *fanegas* (666 liters, 19 bushels)
Carga	4 *fanegas* (222 liters, 6 bushels)
Fanega	12 *celemines* (55 liters, 1.575 bushel)
Celemin	12 *cucharas* (4 and ½ liters, 4 dry quarts)

Wine Measures

Moyo	16 *cantaras* (258 liters, 64 gallons)
Cantara⎱ *Arroba*⎰	8 *azumbres* (16.13 liters, 15.65 in Seville)
Azumbre	4 *cuartillos* (2 liters, ½ gallon)
Cuartillo	(1 pint)

Weights

Tonelada	20 *quintales* (2,000 pounds)
Quintal	4 *arrobas* (100 pounds)
Arroba	25 *libras* (25 pounds)
Libra	16 *onzas* (1 pound, 460 grams)
Onza	(1 ounce, 28 and ¾ grams)

mately six tenths of a cent, and according to Morison seven tenths, both estimations being based on the pre-1934 dollar. In terms of 1975, its value would be about double ($0.013).[42]

The *marco* (230 grams or half a pound) was the measure used to weigh and value bullion and precious metals. In the case of gold, the *marco* was divided into 50 *doblas* or *castellanos* (of 46 decigrams each). Their value varied according to their percentage of fine metal, which was calculated in *quilates* (carats). In 1506 one *quilate* was estimated at 20.4 maravedis per *dobla*. That year Juan de la Cosa brought back a large shipment of gold which was assayed and melted in Seville by the officials of the House of Trade. A kettle drum's content of gold was assayed at 19¼ *quilates* and valued at 395 maravedis per *dobla* (or castellano). A hatchet was assayed at 9¼ *quilates* and sold for 189¼ maravedis per *dobla*. Some *granalla* (fine grain) estimated 19 *quilates* sold for 385 maravedis per *dobla*. This gave the *dobla* (or *castellano*) of pure gold (24 *quilates*) a potential value of 490 maravedis. Therefore, a pound (or 2 *marcos,* or 100 *doblas*) of fine gold would be worth 49,000 maravedis.[43]

Paralleling this, for commercial transactions, a gold coin also called *dobla* or *castellano* was used. It weighed 45.5 decigrams of 23¾ *quilates* and was worth 480 maravedis. There were 50 of these *castellanos* to the *marco.* Other gold coins existed also, emitted by previous kings, and the situation was confusing.

In 1497 the Catholic Sovereigns, wishing to unify the monetary system of Spain, created a new gold coin, the *excelente de Granada,* worth 375 maravedis. There were 65⅓ *excelentes* to the *marco,* and each weighed 34.8 decigrams. The new coin was divided into 11 silver *reals* (worth 34 maravedis each), 375 *maravedis* and 750 *blancas,* but its name, *excelente de Granada,* did not stick. It was soon changed to *ducado,* because of its similarity with the Venetian piece bearing that name. In the sixteenth century, the *ducado* became the standard gold coin, and it maintained its parity throughout the reign of Carlos V, who ruled Spain from 1516 to 1556.[44]

3 The Andalusian Voyages

Alonso de Hojeda, a native of Cuenca, was the son of Rodrigo de Huete, a member of the local nobility. Rodrigo had rallied to the cause of Isabel when she was proclaimed queen of Castile at the death of her brother Enrique IV in 1474, and he had distinguished himself at the two sieges of Madrid (first the town, then the castle), in March— May 1476. But while he was away serving his Queen, the partisans of Enrique's daughter, Juana "La Beltraneja," took advantage of Rodrigo's absence, seized his cattle, horses and sheep, plundered his houses and barns, and even carried off the titles to his lands. He applied to Isabel for help, and through a *real cédula* dated 20 December 1476, she ordered Juan Davila, chief magistrate of Cuenca, to start an inquiry, punish the culprits, and restore to Rodrigo all his stolen property.[1]

Isabel and her husband Fernando never forgot the services rendered them by the father, and they took his son Alonso under their protection. To account for the royal protection, there is no need to suppose that he was the first cousin and protégé of an influential namesake, the inquisitor Alonso de Hojeda, for there is no proof of it; nor is there any need to suppose that he attracted the Queen's attention with his acrobatic feats, by standing on a gargoyle or on a beam sticking out from the Giralda. Being a *criado* (page or retainer) of the royal pair naturally gained him other protectors, like the duke of Medinaceli and Bishop Juan Rodríguez de Fonseca. He was also on good terms with the Chirinos, a Cuenca family who had moved to Andalusia and had changed its name to Valera.[2]

Why did he call himself Hojeda? It may have been his mother's maiden name, for we know that he had a nephew called Pedro de Hojeda, who accompanied him on his second voyage. Using the mother's family name was a frequent occurrence at the time. In spite of his small stature Alonso was a tough and unscrupulous character. He had proved his mettle fighting the Indians in Hispaniola, and he was to prove it again in this forthcoming voyage.

The text of the capitulation Hojeda received from Fonseca has been lost. No doubt, it must have included the usual prohibition to go to the lands discovered by Columbus or belonging to the King of Portugal. According to one source, Hojeda and Peralonso Niño were to sail together; but they quarreled.[3] Hojeda teamed with La Cosa and Amerigo Vespucci; while Niño associated with the Guerras.

Hojeda left with three ships, but only one was under his direct command, the other two having been outfitted by Amerigo at his own expense. The connection between the two navigators must have been very loose, each keeping control of his ship or ships and of his booty, both sailing in the same general direction, but each being free to indulge in side trips. This is the kind of arrangement Vélez de Mendoza made with Luis Guerra one year later.

We shall not here go into the question whether Amerigo Vespucci had already made a voyage of discovery in 1497, for it is beyond the scope of this study. I leave it to Vespucci experts to solve this problem, which has baffled historians on both sides of the Atlantic. There is no proof that he did or did not, since there is no record of his whereabouts from February 1496 to 14 May 1499, when the Florentine empowered his future brother-in-law Martín de Cerezo to represent him in court during the voyage he was about to make with Hojeda.[4]

The armada left the Puerto de Santa María on 18 May 1499, in the morning. The night before, Hojeda's men, a tough bunch, hijacked a bergantin in the harbor, to add to their one caravel; but they were not satisfied, and on the coast of Morocco and Mauritania they looked for other prey. Near the Cabo de Aguer, they captured a caravel, threw out the crew, except for the master and the mate who were the owners and agreed to join the expedition. Hojeda gave the command of the new vessel to *Don* Hernando de Guevara, his *criado* (protégé), a real blueblood since only members of the most aristocratic families could use the title of *Don*.

In the Canaries, which they visited next, Hojeda's men committed various acts of piracy, if we can trust the testimonies of two members of the armada who deserted a few months later in Hispaniola and testified against their chief.[5] In Lanzarote, they broke into houses and barns belonging to the hereditary ruler of the island, Doña Inez Peraza, and they seized cables, anchors, rigging, food, and other supplies, without paying anything. From Gomera, the armada sailed first west and then south. After twenty-four days of navigation, land was sighted 200 leagues east of Paria (according to Hojeda),[6] probably on the coast of Surinam or French Guyana, at a latitude of 5° or 6°N. Some historians think the landstrike may have been near Cape Orange, at the mouth of the Oyajok, at 4°N. There the expedition split. Hojeda, with his two ships, raced (*corrió*) toward Paria, apparently without making any landings, while Vespucci cast anchor a league from shore, planning to disembark. To avoid being drawn into the Vespucci controversy, and wishing to remain as far as possible on solid grounds, we will rely mostly on the Florentine's letter to Lorenzo di Medici (18 July 1500), and refrain from using more questionable material.[7] This way we hope to get a clearer picture of Amerigo's participation in the Hojeda—La Cosa voyage.

Wishing to take a look at the land, but afraid of running into shoals, Vespucci left his ships at anchor, and with about six men in each shallop, rowed all day along the shore. They were amazed at the luxuriance of the tropical forest—so dense that it kept them from landing—at the height of the trees, at the greenness and fragrance of the foliage. Having been unable to find a landing place, they returned to their vessels and decided to try their luck elsewhere. The following day, they set sail southeastward, since Vespucci was anxious to reach Cattigara, southeasternmost point of the Asiatic mainland on the Ptolemy maps; for Amerigo identified South America with Asia, and thought he could reach India: "We pointed our prows southward since it was my intention to see whether I could turn a headland which Ptolemy calls the Cape of Cattigara, which connects with the Sinus Magnus. In my opinion, we were not a great distance from it, according to computed longitude and latitude."[8]

On the way, they saw two huge rivers, one flowing west-east (the Amazon), and the other south-north (the Para). The first was 16 miles wide at its principal channel. As far as 25 miles from shore the sea water was as fresh as stream water, and they filled their casks with it.

Vespucci again left his ships, taking 20 men with him and enough food for four days. They entered one of the rivers with their boats, rowing 18 leagues and making many attempts to land; but they were prevented from doing so because of the shallowness at the banks, and

the denseness of the forest, so thick that a bird could scarcely fly between the branches. They saw signs that the land was inhabited, even
though they were in a torrid zone. This disproved a century-old misconception that tropical regions could not be lived in because of the
heat of the sun. They also noticed a bizarre assemblage of grotesque
birds with baroque features, like the toucan, and many varieties of
parrots with the most diversified plumage. The birds sang melodi-
ously and the air was so fragrant that Vespucci fancied he was in
the Terrestrial Paradise. And the rivers swarmed with many kinds
of fish.

After two days, they interrupted their boat ride and returned to
their ships. They set sail again in the same direction (east-southeast)
for 40 leagues. Then they ran into a strong adverse current, and they
could no longer proceed. This obstacle that stood in their way was the
northern branch of the Southern Equatorial Current, which after reaching the Brazilian elbow races up the northeast coast at speeds varying
from 40 to 80 miles a day. To get out of it, they veered and sailed
north, then northwest.

By that time they had crossed the equator and had lost sight of
Polaris. Amerigo claims that they went as far as 6° south, that is just
below Cape São Roque, on the Brazilian elbow, but this can be doubted.
The Florentine spent sleepless nights watching the southern constellations, unable to locate a star that would move within 10 degrees of the
pole. His quadrant and astrolabe failed him, and however hard he
tried, he was unable to make an exact calculation of his latitude. He
probably did not go beyond 3° south. If he turned back some 40
leagues after leaving the estuary of the Para, then he must have done
so in the vicinity of the Bay of Turiaçu, at a latitude of about 2° S.
While he was in the equatorial zone (July 1499), he could not notice
any perceptible difference between the length of day and night; they
were of equal duration.

Meanwhile, Hojeda had raced all the way to Trinidad, where he
found traces of Columbus's passage one year earlier, on the northeast
shore, next to the Boca del Dragón. Then he visited Paria and landed
on Margarita. Columbus had discovered and baptized the island, without disembarking on it. Hojeda and La Cosa, however, were not the
first to land on Margarita, since they had been preceded there by
Peralonso Niño and Cristóbal Guerra, who, although they had left

Spain two weeks later after Hojeda, had sailed directly to Paria and had beaten him to the Costa de las Perlas.

When and where did Amerigo catch up with Hojeda? We have seen how he had been forced to turn back on the coast of Brazil and had set sail toward the northwest. He reached Trinidad where he went ashore with 21 men. Amerigo puts the island correctly at a latitude of 10°N. In his letter he gives a description of the natives. They were of average size, of yellowish brown color, entirely naked, and good archers, their only arms being bows and arrows. They practiced cannibalism, and Vespucci saw skulls and bones of their victims. They did not eat people of their own tribe; but in their canoes they went to other islands for their supply of human flesh. They received the Spaniards well, took them to one of their villages two leagues away from shore, and gave them plenty of food; but they did so more out of fear than friendship.

The Christians stayed only one day and returned to their ships. The following day, they visited other villages on the south shore. They were so well treated and so well supplied with food that they gave up the idea of kidnapping some of those hospitable natives.

Moving to Paria, which Hojeda had already left, Vespucci anchored at the mouth of a river near a large settlement. He and his men were received by the Indians, who led them into their homes and treated them to many fruits of different kinds and to wine made of fruit juice. The natives also gave them a number of pearls, eleven of which were of good size. They volunteered to bring them more if the Christians would only wait a few days, but Vespucci was in a hurry. Apparently his haste was due to his desire to overtake Hojeda as soon as possible. He and his men left with a load of parrots, and a fond memory of the fine welcome they had received. They set sail again, racing through the Cariaco Trench, from Araya Point to Cape Codera, far from the coast. Thus they don't seem to have had any contact with the Niño-Guerra expedition who stuck close to the shore, bartering with the natives.

It appears that Amerigo caught up with Hojeda and La Cosa before reaching Cape Codera, because all the events mentioned from then on in the *lettera* apply to all four vessels. F. J. Pohl does not think so: "All the facts we know show that Amerigo's two ships were not in consort with the two ships of Hojeda and La Cosa from their land fall in June to their arrival in Española." Yet we have proof that Hojeda's men took part in the battle at Puerto Flechado, which the Florentine describes at length in his letter.[9]

After Cape Codera, several landings were made and usually met with stiff resistance; for the naked Indians of this "costa de gente brava," armed only with bows and arrows, tried to hold their ground against the helmeted and breastplated Spaniards, who cut them to ribbons with their steel swords. The battles usually ended in frightful slaughter. "It often happened that sixteen of us fought against two thousands of them, and at the end we routed them and massacred many of them and pillaged their houses."[10] One such encounter took place at *Aldea Vencida* (Conquered Village), which Hojeda himself identified with Codera Harbor.

Another battle was fought at *Puerto Flechado* (Port of Arrows), in the vicinity of Chichiriviche according to Navarrete. There the Spaniards landed. As a protection against arrows each man wore his armor, and the boats had top covers. The enemies were so numerous that at one time the Christians retreated toward the shore, trying to escape; but a fifty-five-year-old sailor, who had been left to guard the boats, jumped ashore, praying to God and urging the Spaniards to resist. Then, sword in hand, he entered the mêlée, and the Christians following his example turned around and routed the Indians, killing 150 and burning many of their houses. In this fight, one Spaniard died and twenty-one were wounded. The armada remained there twenty days to allow the wounded to recover.

Leaving the continent, the armada visited the Curaçao archipelago. Eleven Christians landed on the largest of the islands, 13 leagues from *tierra firme*. They followed a trail inland, and two and half miles from shore, they found a village of 12 houses, deserted except for seven women so tall that each of them towered over the 11 Spaniards by at least 13 inches. At first the ladies seemed frightened, but the one who appeared to be their leader had the others serve refreshments to the visitors. The latter decided to kidnap two of the women who were approximately 15 years of age, as a present for King Fernando; but as they were about to carry out their plan, 36 natives entered the house where the Christians were being entertained. Each of the newcomers kneeling was taller than Amerigo standing, and their bodies were proportioned to their size. "Each of the women appeared as Pantasilea, and each of the men as Antaeus," remarked Vespucci, who, like any cultured Florentine, was well acquainted with classical mythology. At the sight of the Indian giants, who came in with their bows and arrows and carrying paddles with sword-thin edges, some of the Christians lost their composure, thinking their last hour had come. A conversation started, mostly through sign language. The Spaniards made every effort to appear as men of good will engaged on a world tour, and they carefully avoided any controversial subject. At the first opportunity they took their leave and went back to their ship; but the natives insisted on accompanying them until they embarked.[11]

On this island, the Christians noticed a great quantity of brazilwood. As a result of their visit to Curaçao, it became known as the Island of the Giants and as Brazil Island. Juan de la Cosa, chief pilot of the expedition, labeled it on his famous world map "Y. de brasil-Gigan," thus using both names. La Cosa and Vespucci were not the only ones to see "giants" on South America's north shore. Yañez Pinzón "found" some more, six months later, near Cape São Roque.

After Curaçao, the armada reached another island ten leagues away, where the inhabitants lived in houses built on stilts, as in Venice; hence, the name *Venezuela* (Little Venice), which was given to this whole region by cartographers and which has stuck to this day. At first the natives refused to let the intruders enter their homes; but the latter used force, slashing with their swords the poor Indians who had never seen before weapons that could do so much damage. In the houses the Spaniards found much cotton and noticed that the beams were made of brazilwood. They took great quantities of both cotton and dyewood, and went back to their ships. Cotton grew wild in the countryside, and there was plenty of it.

The island described above has been identified as Aruba; but it could be as well the *Paraguana* peninsula, which can be very easily mistaken for an island, since its only connection with the mainland is a very narrow isthmus. We know, moreover, that the Spaniards discovered Paraguana, for they baptized the northernmost point of that peninsula *Cabo de San Román* on that saint's day (9 August). The inhabitants, the Caquetio Indians, did live in stilted houses, at least during the rainy season.

After going around Paraguana, the expedition sailed southwest and entered a gulf that communicates through a narrow strait with a bay or

large lake (Maracaibo Lake). Because it was the 24th of August, the
Spaniards called it *Lago de San Bartolomé.* There they kidnapped or
obtained through barter some young native wenches. The women of
Maracaibo were very attractive according to sixteenth century chroniclers.

Coming out of the gulf called *Golfo de Venezuela,* the expedition
reached the Guajira peninsula to the west, and saw a cape that they
named *Cabo de la Vela.* There Hojeda acquired a young Indian girl
whom he took to Spain, where she was baptized Isabel. She seems to
have been the daughter or sister of a cacique. He brought her back with
him three years later, to use her as an interpreter and guide. He appears
to have been very fond of her. More will be said about her when we
discuss Hojeda's next voyage.

The territory that Hojeda discovered in this voyage ranged from
Cabo Codera to Cabo de la Vela. On maps and in official documents it
became known as *Coquibacoa* or *Arquibacoa.* In 1501 the Catholic
Sovereigns appointed Hojeda governor of Coquibacoa and granted him
another license for discovery.

From the Cabo de la Vela, the armada sailed to Yaquimo, on the
south coast of Hispaniola, where they arrived on 5 September after a
five-day crossing. This means that they left Guajira on the last day of
August or on the first of September. How, then, are we to explain the
presence on the La Cosa map of a landmark named after *Santa Eufemia*
whose feast day is 16 September? This is the last place-name on the
map west of Cabo de la Vela, and it must mark the farthest point on
the coast explored by the expedition. It seems likely that one or two
ships remained behind after Hojeda's departure, probably Amerigo's
two vessels, continuing the exploration of the coast toward the west for
two or three more weeks, before joining the rest of the fleet. Since
Vespucci writes that it took him seven days to cross over to Hispaniola,
he could not have overtaken Hojeda until 23 September at the earliest.

Why did the expedition make port at Yaquimo, instead of returning
directly to Spain? Vespucci gives the most plausible explanation: the
ships had become unseaworthy, and they leaked so badly that their
pumps could scarcely keep them afloat. They had to be careened and
repaired, and Hispaniola was the closest place where labor skilled in
this sort of work could be found. Besides, the men were exhausted and
needed rest, and supplies were low.[12] Nevertheless, in Santo Domingo,

Columbus and his officials thought otherwise. Their first reaction, when they learned of Hojeda's arrival, was that he had gone there to load brazilwood; for Yaquimo (today Jacmel in southern Haiti) was also known as Port Brazil. The countryside around it was rich in dyewood, which could not be cut without a special license from the Crown.

At the time Hojeda landed, Columbus had just made peace with Francisco Roldán, giving in to most of his demands, and the latter was in control of all the southwest portion of the island; but discontent was still brewing among the settlers. Columbus sent Roldán with three caravels to Yaquimo, with orders to prevent Hojeda from cutting brazilwood. When Roldán arrived (29 September), Hojeda was no longer there. He had sent his ships farther west, and he made his quarters in the village of a cacique named Haniguayaba, to bake bread and obtain other supplies. Learning of Roldán's approach, he went to meet him with five or six men. Roldán upbraided him for landing in Yaquimo without first visiting the Admiral and asking for his authorization. The navigator answered that he had been forced to do so because his vessels needed repair and his crew needed food. As the alcalde further questioned him, he explained that he had been given a license to discover by the King and Queen, but could not show it to him since he had left it in his caravel. It was his intention to pay his respects to the Admiral and discuss with him some things that concerned him. In the course of his conversation with Roldán, Hojeda gave him an inkling of Columbus' disgrace and pending removal from office; for as he was about to sail from Spain on his voyage of discovery, Fernando and Isabel had decided to appoint Bobadilla governor of Hispaniola, and the latter's arrival was only a matter of time.

Apparently satisfied with Hojeda's explanation, the alcalde let him go back to the village where he was making bread; but before reporting to Columbus he did some checking. He made his way to the harbor where Hojeda's caravel was anchored. There La Cosa showed him the capitulation signed by Bishop Fonseca. Persuaded now that the discoverer meant well, Roldán set out to report to the Admiral.

When Hojeda finished his food gathering, he raised anchor; but instead of going to Santo Domingo to pay his respects to Columbus, he sailed toward the west, rounded Cape Tiburon, and took shelter in Xaragua Bay, where he had his ships careened. The Europeans in the area gave him a big welcome, sharing with him not what they had, but what the Indians had, this being the kind of generosity that prevailed among the settlers of Hispaniola according to Las Casas.[13] They were discontented because they had not been paid the stipend they had been promised before leaving Spain, and they cursed "the Admiral of the Mosquitoes." Hojeda took advantage of this widespread unrest, claiming he could collect from Columbus the sums due them. He even asserted that the Sovereigns had given him power to do so, and he talked as if he could blackmail or force the Genoese into making good the royal promise. Perhaps he was really trying to blackmail Columbus for his own end, since he was not a scrupulous man; or possibly he had been given secret instructions to undermine the Admiral's authority to make it easier to dismiss him. When Hojeda left Spain (18 May, 1499), Fernando and Isabel had already decided to replace Columbus, and their letter notifying him of his removal was signed on 26 May 1499. Yet Bobadilla (with the letter) did not leave Spain until July 1500, one month after Hojeda's return. Was this part of a preconceived plan? Was it decided to wait for Hojeda's arrival and find from him the true state of affairs in Hispaniola? Or was it more coincidence? Did it really take Bobadilla fourteen months to prepare for his mission?

In Xaragua, Hojeda began spreading stories, some true, some false. He even asserted that the Queen was dying and that this meant the end of the regime instituted by Columbus. He had not expected to find the Genoese and Roldán reconciled, and the latter's followers were hostile to him. There was an armed clash, which proved indecisive but resulted in some bloodshed.

As he was returning from Santo Domingo to Xaragua, Roldán learned what had happened. When he arrived, Hojeda and his men had already taken refuge on their ships. Roldán wrote a letter proposing an interview and sent Diego de Escobar, one of his lieutenants, to deliver it; but Escobar could not persuade Hojeda to agree to the proposed meeting. Roldán sent another messenger, Diego de Trujillo, who fared worse than Escobar, for as he came on board, he was arrested and put in irons. A third Roldán follower was also captured by the partisans of Hojeda, who threatened to hang his two prisoners unless a deserter, a one-armed man called Juan Pintor, was returned to him. Then he raised anchor and moved to Cahay, another harbor in Xaragua Bay.

The wily Roldán did not give up and resorted to strategy. He followed Hojeda by land and once more proposed an interview, suggesting that it be held on Hojeda's caravel. This time the latter agreed and sent a bergantin to pick him up, with the condition that Roldán could not bring with him more than half a dozen men. As soon as the alcalde and his escort embarked, they jumped, sword in hand, on the eight sailors who manned the boat and were busy with their oars. At this signal, other Roldán followers who were hiding in the woods nearby came rushing to the beach, and in no time they captured the bergantin and its crew. This was an humiliating blow for Hojeda, and the loss of his boat hampered his return to Spain. He and La Cosa got into a bark and approached the landing where Roldán stood, and a conversation started as soon as they were within hearing distance of each other. Hojeda offered to free the two men he had threatened to hang if the bergantin was returned to him. Roldán agreed. After this episode, Hojeda made himself scarce. According to Las Casas, he sailed back and forth, going on *cabalgatas* (raids) to Puerto Rico and other adjacent islands, and to other sections of Hispaniola, to load his ships with Indian slaves, leaving once and for all in February or March 1500.

After his departure an investigation was ordered by Columbus. Two of the main witnesses were deserters from the armada, the sailor Juan Velásquez and the *cirujano* (surgeon) Master Alonso. The latter was from Huete, a small town in Cuenca province, therefore, a *paisano* (compatriot) of Hojeda; but he had turned sour on his chief. He and Velásquez accused Hojeda of inciting the Indians to rebel, of trading with them and giving arms to some of them. The most interesting feature of this inquiry is that it reveals the names of some thirty participants in the expedition, who served on the two caravels directly under Hojeda's command. Here is the list of the officers who are mentioned in this document:[14]

Caravela Mayor
captain: Alonso de Hojeda
master and pilot: Juan Vizcaino (La Cosa)
mate: Nicola Veneciano
cooper: Simon Ginovés
caulker: Pedro de Laredo
apothecary: Master Bernal

surgeon: Master Alonso, who deserted
assistant pilot: Diego Martin Chamorro (Vicente Yañez Pinzón's
brother-in-law)

Caravela taken on the coast of Africa
captain: Don Fernando Ladrón de Guevara
master and part owner: unnamed, killed in Hispaniola
pilot: Juan López
mate and part owner: Pero Mateos

This list of participants in the voyage raises two interesting problems. The first concerns a man who is included in it; the second is
about a man it does not mention.

1. The captain of the second caravel is listed as *Don* Fernando (or
Hernando) de Guevara, the scion of a most aristocratic family, whose
education as a caballero and a soldier had been entrusted to Hojeda.
Don Hernando also served with his tutor as ship captain in 1502, during Hojeda's second voyage. It so happened that just after the expedition left Hispaniola (February–March 1500), a troublemaker named
Don Hernando de Guevara kidnapped or seduced the beautiful Hi-
gueymota, daughter of Princess Anacona and niece of the cacique
Behechio, vaguely promising to marry her. It was rumored that Hi-
gueymota had been Franciso Roldán's mistress, and the alcalde, angered, ordered Guevara to stay away from the girl. Don Hernando
promised; but he felt deeply humiliated, and he plotted to kill Roldán.
The latter was warned, however. He trapped his would-be murderer
and handed him over to Columbus, who had him jailed. At that time,
another troublemaker and cousin of Don Hernando, Adrian de
Muxica, raised a small band of followers to rescue his kinsman and
kill both Columbus and Roldán. He too was captured and later
executed (June–July 1500). Don Hernando was still in jail, waiting to
be hanged, when Bobadilla landed (23 August), arrested Columbus,
and freed the prisoners.

The problem we are trying to solve is the following: were there
two Don Hernando de Guevaras or just one? Did the ship's captain,
tired of a seaman's life, leave his vessel and go native? Or perhaps he
may have been left behind by Hojeda to stir up trouble; after his narrow escape, he may have gone back to Spain and rejoined his chief.
This is unlikely. Las Casas, who knew the rebel quite well, gives the

impression that he was a discontented settler. His remark, "I don't
remember if Don Hernando, whom I knew well . . . took part in the
Roldán rebellion," implies that Hernando the black sheep was already
in Hispaniola before Hojeda landed there (5 September 1499), since
before that date Francisco Roldán had come to terms with the Admiral
and his rebellion had ended.[15] Therefore, we can safely assume that
there were two Don Hernando de Guevaras, most likely related but
very different in behavior, one being a ship's captain and the other a
discontented settler.

2. The absence of the pilot Bartolomé Roldán from the list of crew
members also poses some problems. Las Casas declares that "Hojeda
took with him the pilot Bartolomé Roldán whose name was often
mentioned in Santo Domingo, and we all knew him."[16] In addition, a
witness in the *Pleitos,* Jacome Ginovés, declared in his testimony that
he saw Bartolomé Roldán with Hojeda in Yaquimo, when the latter
arrived from tierra firme.[17] On the strength of these two assertions,
most historians have been of the opinion that Bartolomé Roldán accompanied Hojeda and La Cosa in their 1499–1500 voyage. Yet we
have Bartolomé's own testimony, given in 1513 in the *Pletios,* that he
sailed with Diego de Lepe in 1499–1500. Of course Bartolomé was
much in demand as a pilot; but he cannot have been in two places at
once. We find the solution to this dilemma in his answer to a question
that was put to him on 10 November 1513, in the *Pleitos.* He was
asked "if he knows that at that time Alonso de Hojeda and the pilot
Juan de la Cosa and those who went with them discovered on the coast
of Tierra Firme toward the West . . . as far as the land called Coqui-
boca." His answer was that he heard Hojeda and La Cosa say so ("que
oyo decir lo contenido en la dicha pregunta a los dichos Hojeda e Juan
de la Cosa").[18] If he heard of it from Hojeda and La Cosa, if his
knowledge of their discovery of Coquibacoa was purely hearsay, then
he did not take part in that discovery and in their 1499–1500 voyage.
Jacome Ginovés probably confused Bartolomé Roldán with Francisco
Roldán, for the latter came to Yaquimo to see Hojeda. As for Las
Casas, who wrote of these events some forty years later, his memory
must have failed him.

The fact that in the investigation ordered by Columbus no mention
is made of Vespucci and his men is ample proof that the Florentine
had no part in Hojeda's antics, carefully avoided making trouble, and

even entertained cordial relations with the Admiral. They became good friends after both returned to Spain, where Columbus died in 1506.

In his *lettera*, Amerigo declares that it took him 67 days to cross the ocean and reach the Azores, where his crews supplied themselves with food. From there, because of contrary winds, they had to sail to the Canaries, and from the Canaries to Madeira, and from Madeira to Cadiz. In so doing they must have spent at least a month; which means that their return trip lasted three or four months. On the other hand, we know that they reached Spain about 18 June 1500, for Amerigo wrote to Lorenzo di Medici on 18 July "to give news of my return a month ago," and he added that his voyage lasted thirteen months, which adds up exactly to 18 June 1500, since they had left Spain on 18 May 1499.[19] Now if their return trip took them three or four months, and if they arrived in mid-June, their departure from Hispaniola must have taken place in February or March, as Las Casas stated in his *Historia*.[20]

One apparent discordant note in Vespucci's letter: he mentions that his stay in Hispaniola lasted only two months; while according to Las Casas, Hojeda was there six months from 5 September 1499, to February–March 1500. The difference between these two statements can be explained. First of all, the Florentine stayed behind on *Tierra Firme* after Hojeda sailed for Yaquimo, for on 16 September he was still at Santa Eufemia, a spot west of Cabo de la Vela. He may not have caught up with Hojeda until October. Second, the two months he stayed in Hispaniola probably correspond to the time Hojeda was stirring trouble and playing hide and seek with Franciso Roldán (October–November?). Then, after the alcalde outwitted him, Hojeda began his *cabalgatas* (raids) on other islands, slave hunting, keeping on the move, and staying out of Hispaniola most of the time. This probably took place in December 1499–February 1500. Both Las Casas and Amerigo declare that the leaders of the expedition agreed to capture batches of Indians and load them on their ships to sell them as slaves. According to the Dominican, these acts of piracy took place in Puerto Rico, other adjacent islands, and some sections of the coast of Hispaniola, while Amerigo situates them farther north, in the Bahamas. Finally, there must have been a final stopover for food and supplies in Hispaniola. Therefore, the four vessels forming the armada left the West Indies together and reached Cadiz together.

I know that many historians do not agree with this and think that Hojeda preceded Vespucci by two months or more. We have seen that Amerigo reached Spain in mid-June 1500; but so did Hojeda, and we shall try to prove it. On 5 June, Alonso Vélez de Mendoza was granted a license that forbade him to go to the lands discovered by Columbus and Cristobal Guerra. Since no mention is made of Hojeda, this means that his discoveries were not yet known in Spain and he had not yet returned. One and a half months later, on 20 and 22 July, Vélez and his backers were read a revised text of the capitulation, in which Hojeda's name had been added to those of Columbus and Cristóbal Guerra. Therefore Hojeda must have returned during that six weeks' period, very likely in mid-June like Vespucci.

When the armada arrived at Cadiz, the Indians it had brought were offered for sale. There were a total of 200 out of 235 who must have been loaded on all four caravels, since Amerigo's two ships, with a crew of less than 30 each, could not have exceeded 60 tons and could not have carried alone such a large number of captives in addition to their own personnel. The other 35 Indians had died during the crossing and their corpses had been thrown overboard. Vespucci's men (55 survivors out of 57 starters) shared a profit of 500 ducats (187,500 maravedis), which meant an average of 3,410 maravedis per man if they all shared equally. In addition to their cargo of human flesh, not much had been brought back, since the expedition had been on the move most of the time, never staying long in one place. Fourteen colored pearls were presented to the Queen. Stones that looked like beryl, emerald, amethyst, also formed part of the loot.[21] The main reason why Vélez and other would-be discoverers were forbidden to go to Coquibacoa (the land discovered by Hojeda) was because the latter had found there *piedras verdes* (emeralds), and the Crown wanted to keep it secret.

Hojeda owed the government the *quinto,* or one fifth of the profits. To pay it, he had to sell the booty he had brought back on his two caravels in order to get some ready cash. Since this took time, he made a part payment, and for the rest he concluded a deal with Rodrigo de Villacorta, treasurer of the Indies. The text of this agreement, certified 22 October 1500 by the notary Francisco de Sigura, reveals the name of Hojeda's father. Because of its importance, we reproduce it here in a slightly condensed form:

"I Alfonso de Fojeda [sic], son of the late Rodrigo de Huete, resident of Cuenca, acknowledge that I owe Rodrigo de Villacorta, treasurer of the Indies of the Ocean Sea for the King and the Queen our Lords . . . 23,797 maravedis which their Highnesses should have from the rest of the quinto due them for the things brought back in the caravels *Condesa* and *Florida,* with which I went to discover in the Indies . . . , to be paid in Seville or in any other city, town or village, between today, date of the signature of this letter, and the 28th of February 1501. . . ."²²

Amerigo must have paid his *quinto* separately. He offered the Queen some beautiful pearls, and she was very pleased with them. Although he had a touch of malaria, he wanted to go back to the Indies. Like him, Hojeda and La Cosa wanted to return, but none of the three would associate with the others, since each had a different plan. Hojeda wanted to go back to *his* land, Coquibacoa, settle there, and become its governor; on 28 July 1500, the Catholic Sovereigns agreed and gave him the customary letter of recommendation to Fonseca. On the other hand, La Cosa wished to explore the coast west of Coquibacoa, beyond Cabo de la Vela, hoping to find there a passage to India. For this he teamed with Rodrigo de Bastidas, who had been granted a capitulation a few weeks before, on the same day as Vélez de Mendoza (5 June). As for Vespucci, he wanted to sail in the opposite direction, to the southeast, and continue his exploration of the coast beyond the Amazon, which he had been forced to interrupt as a result of his encounter with the South Equatorial Current. He still thought that by sailing southeast, he would reach Cape Cattigara, southeasternmost point of Asia according to Ptolemy. Once he had rounded that cape, he felt certain he would get through to *Taprobana* and India.

In the 18 July letter from Seville, Vespucci wrote: "The King is fitting out for me three ships to the end that I may go again to discover. I believe they will be ready by the middle of September."²³ What was the expedition referred to in his letter? Probably that of Vélez de Mendoza and Luis Guerra, which left Seville toward the end of August. It is not wrong to assume that Amerigo contacted Vélez about the possibility of associating with him; and he probably offered to outfit a caravel at his own cost. Then, on 20 August, a coup de théâtre occurred. Vélez was called again before Fonseca and was read an additional clause to his capitulation, forbidding him to admit foreigners in his armada.[24]

The prohibition was evidently aimed at Vespucci, but why? What had happened? Had the Florentine been fooled by the wily Fernando, the King after whom Macchiavelli allegedly fashioned his *Principe?* Or did the Sovereigns and their advisers have a sudden change of heart? Probably they came to think that a foreigner like Amerigo, intelligent, skilled in navigation and in mapmaking, with wealth and powerful friends abroad, could become a danger if he learned more of the "secrets" of the New World.

2   Peralonso Niño and Cristóbal Guerra
      1499–1500

Peralonso Niño was an old hand at transoceanic navigation, for he had accompanied Columbus on his first and second voyages. He had also led convoys taking troops, settlers, and supplies to Hispaniola, being rewarded with the title of *piloto mayor.* Some historians believe that he also took part in the third voyage, which resulted in the discovery of South America; but there is evidence to the contrary. It is true that he volunteered to serve in that voyage as chief pilot, and collected four months' advance pay in December 1497; but soon after that, he went to the Court and did not return.[1] According to the testimony given in 1512 in the *Pleitos de Colón* by Alonso Ruiz, a relative of Peralonso, the latter was still at the Court at the time the discovery of Paria became known, teaching cartography to the Prince (*amostrando a cartear al principe*).[2] This is impossible, however, since Prince Juan, the son of Fernando and Isabel and heir to the throne, had died fourteen months earlier (4 October 1497). Peralonso may have taught the art of map reading to Juan in 1497; but in December 1498 the heir to the throne was Miguel of Portugal, grandson of the Catholic sovereigns, a child of but a few months, much too young to learn cartography. At that time, there was no prince of the blood who could profit from Niño's lessons . . . unless it was the King himself. In the absence of more precise information, it would not be too wrong to infer that Peralonso, like Hojeda and La Cosa, was at the Court in some kind of advisory capacity relating to the Indies.

When Niño began organizing his voyage, he tried to make it, as most did, a family affair. Among the members of his crew we find three of his brothers (Juan, Cristóbal, and Francisco). There was also a son or nephew called Bartolomé Pérez Niño. Peralonso also hired Alonso García and Juan Barrero, two pilots who had been with Columbus in Paria. They knew the route to follow and were already familiar with part of the land to be explored. They must have played a leading role in the voyage. Other crew members whose names have been preserved: Juan Viñas, Francisco Destrada, and Juan Martín Flamenco.

Hiring the crew was probably an easy task for Peralonso, who had been a sailor all his life; but providing the pay, the supplies, and the ship was a much more difficult matter, for he was not a rich man. To obtain the needed funds, he turned to the Guerra brothers, and one of them, Luis, agreed to finance the expedition. Luis was a wealthy *bizcochero;* like his brother Antón, he had been supplying vessels going to America with flour and hardtack. To protect the family interests, he put up one condition: that Cristóbal, the youngest of the three Guerra brothers, should be the captain. Niño did not object, nor did the Crown; and it seems that the capitulation obtained from Fonseca was in Cristóbal's name. At any rate, he received from the Queen the titles of *capitán* and *receptor*.[3] As captain, realizing his own inexperience, he probably let Niño run the caravel much as he pleased; but as receptor of the Queen's *quinto* he was going to make things hot for Niño, and was largely responsible for landing him in jail when they returned to Spain.

Peralonso Niño and Cristóbal Guerra sailed from the Rio Tinto on a 50-ton caravel, with a crew of 33, at the beginning of June 1499, about two weeks after Hojeda and La Cosa had left from the Puerto de Santa Maria (18 May). They followed the same route (Canaries, Cabo Verde archipelago), which was the route Columbus had taken in 1498 and may have traced on his map; but the Niño–Guerra expedition sighted Trinidad before Hojeda and La Cosa, and went through the Boca de la Sierpe and the Boca del Dragón, between Trinidad and the mainland, toward the end of July. In these waters, they encountered a fleet of 18 canoes manned by cannibals who had been hunting for human flesh. The cannibals showered the Spaniards with arrows; but a few cannonballs terrified them and put them to flight, for they had never heard or seen anything like it before. Niño's men managed to seize a dugout in which one cannibal had remained, the others having jumped overboard. In the same canoe was a prisoner, all tied up, probably destined to be eaten. The Spaniards decided to have some fun by reversing the roles. They freed the prisoner and handed over to him the cannibal as his captive. The latter took a fierce beating until he was knocked unconscious.[4]

The Spaniards reached Paria, an elongated and steep peninsula that stretches horizontally, and there they loaded brazilwood. Then they landed on Margarita, an island 41 miles long and 19 wide, divided into two parts: Margarita proper (east), and Mocanao (west), connected by a narrow sandbar. Its twin masses of rough, abrupt mountain, topped by tropical forests, are visible for many miles. There Niño and Guerra found a great quantity of pearls, thus justifying the name given to Margarita by Columbus in 1498, for it means *pearl* in Greek, in addition to being the name of Princess Margaret of Burgundy, after whom Columbus had baptized the island.

The expedition followed the north shore of Paria, rounded Araya Point, entered the Gulf of Cariaco (August), and turned westward. For the next two months (September and October), they sailed along the coast as far as Cape Codera, visiting lands called, from east to west, *Cumana, Maracapana* and *Curiana.* This is the coast that became known as the *Costa de las Perlas.*

Before we go further, we should clarify the location of Curiana, since there have been differences of opinion. Las Casas stretches Curiana as far as Coro, south of the Paraguana peninsula; but according to the capitulation granted Hojeda in 1501, it was included in the Costa de las Perlas and placed east of Cape Codera. In the same document, the limits set for the Costa de las Perlas were in the east the *Frailes,* a small archipelago east of Margarita, and in the west the *Farallón,* a rocky islet north of Cape Codera.

The Spaniards made their first landing near a hamlet of eight houses. Some 50 natives from a village three miles distant, led by their cacique, came to greet them. Attracted by the glittering trinkets the sailors offered them, they exchanged for some brass rings, needles, and glass beads, the pearls they wore on their necks, ears, and noses. In less than an hour the Spaniards thus obtained 15 ounces of pearls. The natives were unafraid and hospitable, since this was their first contact with Europeans. They invited Niño and his men to pay them a visit. The Christians accepted the invitation, and the following morning they anchored near the village; but when they saw the entire population approaching toward them, the Spaniards who were only 33 dared not land, and they motioned to the Indians to come to the ship. Jumping into their dugouts, the natives paddled to the caravel and climbed on board. They all brought pearls for barter, which they readily exchanged for a few trifles. Recovering from their fear, the Spaniards landed, entered the village, and explored the countryside. They spent 20 days there, bartering with the friendly natives, from whom they got food at bargain prices. One dove cost them one needle, a pheasant two, a peacock four. They traded a glass bead for a goose. At first, the Indians, who wore no clothes, did not know what to do with the needles; but after they learned how to use them to remove the splinters from their feet and to pick their teeth, they clamored for more.

Pietro Martire d'Anghiera, who besides being a churchman, was also a man of the Renaissance, keenly interested in human nature, has left a lengthy description of the natives' way of life, which he obtained from Peralonso and other participants in this expedition. The Indians went about naked, except for their genitals which they kept in some sort of gourd held in place by thread. Their houses consisted of sticks of wood dug into the ground, and a roof of palm leaves. They ate the flesh of the oysters from which they extracted the pearls. They also fed on the wild animals that roamed through their forests: wild boar, deer, and hares, which they killed with their arrows, for they were skilled archers. They had no cattle, sheep, or goats; but the women raised various kinds of ducks and geese. Their fields, tilled by the women, produced corn and *cassava* (manioc), from which they made their bread; but the men preferred to hunt, go to war, and dance.

They desiccated the bodies of their dead chiefs by laying them on top of a platform and lighting a slow fire under it. The flesh melted away; but the bones and skin were left intact; and the dried corpses were preserved to be honored by their descendants. Naturally, Pietro Martire could not fail to bring in a comparison with the Roman *penates*.

The natives of the Costa de las Perlas held markets where they sold their products to neighboring tribes, in exchange for pottery and for tiny ornaments made of *guanines* (alloys) that represented little birds or small animals. They hung these ornaments on their pearl earrings and necklaces. In their commercial dealings, they haggled as much as European women did with peddlers.

They had no precious metal to barter with the Spaniards, because they did not produce any. The few gold objects they owned were imported, and they wanted to keep them. They told the Christians that they would find plenty of gold six days' navigation to the west, in a country called *Cauchieta*. Navarrete puts it between Cape Codera and La Guaira. The name of this land was probably derived from the fact that the Caquetio Indians inhabited a great part of it. The Spaniards left Curiana and reached Cauchieta on 1 November. There the natives traded gold willingly since it seemed of no value to them; but they kept the pearls they used as ornaments, for they imported them from Curiana and prized them highly. The Christians also acquired wildcats, some fine-looking monkeys, and parrots of multicolored plumage. In November the country enjoyed a mild climate. Every night the Little Dipper, including the Polar Star, failed to appear. The Spaniards knew they were near the equator, but they could not determine the exact latitude. Las Casas estimated it at 7° or 8° N while it was closer to 10°. There was plenty of cotton, for it grew wild, and the natives used it to make loose-fitting drawers, which formed their whole wardrobe.

The Indians were friendly and unsuspicious. When they saw the caravel come close to shore, they would rush toward it in their dugouts and climb on board day and night, without any fear or distrust; but they were jealous of their women. If some Christians entered their houses, the women would hide outside and gaze at the visitors as if they were superhuman beings.

After spending approximately two months in Cauchieta (November and December), the Spaniards sailed westward to a point farther down the coast; but when they tried to land, they were met by 2,000 naked ferocious-looking men, armed with bows and spears. The Christians motioned out to them that they wished to trade, showing them some of the trinkets they had brought from Spain, but to no avail. The Indians held their ground and kept them from landing.

Such enmity contrasted sharply with the friendly welcome of the other tribes. Why the difference? Probably because the hostile Indians had already received the visit of other Europeans, had come into contact with them, and had suffered from their cruelty and greed. A few months before, Hojeda and La Cosa had been there. Navarrete supposes that the place where Niño and his men were prevented from landing was Chichiriviche, which he identifies with Puerto Flechado, the name given by Hojeda to a beach where he had an encounter with the natives in which 21 of his men were wounded by *flechas* (arrows), and another was killed. Possibly Hojeda had been trying to capture Indians to sell them as slaves. Some 20 years later, after the Spanish conquest, the Dominicans established a monastery in Chichiriviche. Pietro Martire obtained from them a very detailed and most interesting account about the Indians of that town; but since this is not within the scope of the present study, we give it only a passing mention.[5]

After their setback, Niño and Guerra returned to Curiana, glad to be back in friendly territory. They remained there 20 days (January 1500) and obtained a new load of pearls, as beautiful as those of the Orient, but not so well perforated, since the Indians had no iron tools. Some were as big as hazelnuts. When the Spaniards left Curiana, they had acquired 96 pounds of pearls, which they had obtained for trifles worth a few pennies.[6]

They sailed from Curiana on February 6. On their way back, following the coast, they reached Araya Point, at the foot of which marshes fill at high tide with sea water, producing under the tropical sun some of the finest salt in the world. Las Casas himself had several ships loaded with that salt when he was there years later. In the waters around the point, Niño's men noticed an infinite quantity of skates and sardines.[7]

According to Las Casas, as they returned they retraced their steps, going along the coast of Paria, then through the Boca del Dragón and the Boca de la Sierpe; but this is unlikely since Pietro Martire states that their return journey was shorter. They must have sailed directly from Araya Point to Spain, but because of the prevalent easterly trades, they were delayed and it took them 61 days to cover the distance. Then something strange happened. Instead of landing in Andalusia, as the capitulation probably ordered them, they made port at Bayona in Galicia, just north of the Portuguese border (about 10 April). Had they been forced to do so by the weather? Or was it some error in navigation? Or was it an intended "oversight" to avoid paying the royal treasury its due? We don't know; but it is a positive fact that

Peralonso Niño and other members of the expedition hid part of their share of the loot, instead of declaring it to the authorities. Cristóbal Guerra, taking his title of *receptor* seriously, vainly urged them to report all their gain; when they paid no heed, he denounced them to Don Hernando de la Vega, viceroy of Galicia, who had all the cheaters jailed, including Peralonso Niño. The Queen was very indignant at the behavior of some of her subjects. She ordered one of her officials (the name is left blank, but it may have been Fonseca) to go to Bayona, locate the pearls that had been hidden or illegally sold to local merchants, and confiscate them. She also ordered an inquiry to find out who the culprits were and have them properly punished.[8]

Niño was released later but lost the royal favor. Although he kept his title of chief pilot and was sent several times on official missions to Hispaniola, he never took part in any other voyage of discovery. On the other hand, the Queen was very much pleased with Cristóbal Guerra's conduct in this affair. Two months later she decided to send him back to the Costa de las Perlas, hoping that he would bring back another haul of pearls.

The Niño–Guerra voyage of 1499–1500 proved to be a very fruitful venture, and the pearls attracted a great deal of attention. When the expedition returned to Spain, the Court was in Seville, and so was Pietro Martire. At a dinner in the palace of the Duke of Medina Sidonia, he saw 101 ounces of pearls, which had been brought there to tempt the duke into buying them. Martire's comment was the following: "I certainly was glad to see them so beautiful and sparkling."

3   Vicente Yañez Pinzón
      1499–1500

The brothers Pinzón, Martín Alonso and Vicente Yañez, had been with Columbus on his first voyage of discovery. Martín Alonso died soon after his return to Spain; but Vicente Yañez kept navigating for some 20 years, often on official missions. As early as 1495, he was contracted by Juan de Fonseca to serve as captain of two caravels that were to join the armada of Aragón.[1]

On 6 June 1499, Vicente received a license to discover. Since this is the oldest capitulation whose text is known, it deserves close scrutiny. It begins thus: "We Don Juan de Fonseca . . . . in the name of their Majesties, and in virtue of an order and a letter we hold from them, to you Vicente Yañez Pinzón and to those who may associate with you, we give license to go and discover islands and landmasses through the Ocean Sea, and we promise we will truly keep all that is set down and agreed upon in this instruction, which is as follows. . . ."

By the terms of his capitulation, Vicente Yañez was allowed to go anywhere in the Indies, except to the islands or lands already discovered by Columbus, or belonging to the King of Portugal. On each of his ships there should be an appointee of the Crown, whose duty would be to keep an account of anything of value acquired during the voyage. Once the expedition returned to Spain, all the expenses and costs would be deducted from the gross; then the *quinto* would be set aside and paid out to the royal treasury.

Two other clauses forbade bringing back brazilwood and slaves, except negroes or mulattoes "or the kind who can be held as slaves in Spain." Both these clauses were disregarded as we shall see later. No limit was set as to the number of vessels that could be equipped. To outfit them and obtain the necessary supplies, Vicente Yañez was allowed by a letter from Fonseca to take out of the country, free of any export tax, 150 barrels of salt pork, 20 quintals of oil, 40 more of rigging, 4 rolls of dyed fabrics, 7 rolls of rough woolen material and 20 more of sail canvass (5 August 1499); but Gutierre de Prado, *almojarife* (chief customs officer) of Seville, kept insisting on the payment of the export tax, and on 22 October, Yañez had an injunction issued to Gutierre de Prado. Yet the latter would not give in. He alleged that some of the items Yañez and his backers were loading on their ships were not included in Fonseca's letter, such as olives, mirrors, hawk-bells, etc. . . . and he kept insisting on the payment of the export tax until an order came from the Court (7 November). The texts of the injunction, Prado's rejoinder, the capitulation, and Fonseca's letter, have been preserved in the records of the notary public Gonzalo Bernal de la Becerra. Professor Antonio Muro Orejón found them there some 30 years ago and published them.[2]

Vicente Yañez sailed with four ships. We know the names of three of the pilots: Juan de Umbria, Juan de Xerez, and Juan Quintero. A physician named García Fernández doubled as *escrivano,* or clerk appointed by the government. Yañez Pinzón was joined by one brother-in-law (Diego Martín) and by at least four nephews (Juan and Francisco Martín, Arias Pérez, and Diego Fernández). Other sailors were: Antón Hernández Colmenero, Diego Prieto, Pedro Ramírez, Manuel Valdovinos, Juan Calvo, Juan de Palencia, Cristóbal de Vega, Diego de Alfaro, García Alonso, and García Hernández de Huelva. Their names appear in the *Pleitos,* and Professor Muro mentions them in his article. To this list should be added the name Pedro Medel, another witness in the *Pleitos.*[3]

According to Pietro Martire, the expedition left Palos about 1 December 1499.[4] It sailed through the Canaries and stopped over in Santiago Island (in Cabo Verde archipelago), from which it sailed on 13 January 1500. Then it followed a south-southwest direction for some 300 leagues, until the North Star disappeared from the sky. The Spaniards remained for some time without noticing either of the two polar constellations. They attributed this to the existence of a ridge which separated both hemispheres and made it impossible to see the South Polar Star until that ridge had been crossed. Columbus had expressed similar views on October 1498, in a letter to the Catholic Sovereigns.[5]

On 26 January 1500, they saw land and sailed toward a cape on the northeast corner of Brazil. They called it *Cape Consolation.* It has been identified as Cape São Roque (5° S.), although some historians think otherwise.[6] The water around it was muddy and had a whitish color. The Spaniards took soundings and found the bottom at 16 fathoms. They landed northwest of it, at a place they called *Rostro Hermoso,* noticed human tracks but saw no one for two days. Yañez took possession of the land for Castile, following the usual procedure of pacing back and forth, drinking water from a stream, cutting down branches, carving his name and those of the King and Queen on rocks and on tree trunks. One morning they made their way to a spot where they had seen a fire burning at night, and found a tribe camping not far from their landing place. Yañez dispatched 40 armed men toward the encampment, and the Indians in turn sent 32 of their number, armed with bows and arrows and apparently determined to fight. The Christians tried to cajole them and induce them to trade, offering them hawkbells, mirrors, glass beads, etc., but the natives showed no interest, and their attitude became more threatening. They looked bigger than Germans or Hungarians, and their footprints were twice the average size. The Spaniards refrained from attacking. Finally both sides withdrew, the Christians to their ships, and the natives to their fire; but during the night, the latter decamped and disappeared. These savages were later described to Pietro Martire by members of the expedition as gypsylike nomads who move from one country to another at harvest time.

Sailing again west-northwest, the Spaniards reached the mouth of a shallow river, where they anchored their ships. Then they went upstream in their boats to contact the natives and examine the land. Soon they saw on a hilltop a crowd of naked people, toward whom Yañez dispatched a well-armed man as a messenger, to engage in a friendly conversation. Trying to break the ice and arouse their curiosity, the sailor threw at them a hawkbell, and they in turn cast in his direction a gilded stick of two *palmos* (16 inches), probably made of cheap alloy. Believing that all is gold that glitters, the man stooped to pick it up, and the Indians jumped him, but he, with his buckler and sword, defended himself so well that his companions were able to rush to his rescue. The natives stood their ground and showered the Christians with their arrows, killing about ten of them. Then taking the offensive, they rushed to the riverbank and tried to seize the boats. They killed the guardian of one of them, leaving his body riddled with arrows; but the Spaniards regained the upper hand, with their spears and swords slashing and slaughtering the savages who had no protection other than their bare skins.

Saddened by the loss of their companions, the Christians sailed again, following the coast, and some 40 leagues to the northwest, they found a stretch of sea where the water was as fresh as stream water, in spite of the fact that they were 30 to 40 miles from land. They filled their empty casks and headed toward the shore. They saw many islands, which appeared green and fertile, with a dense population of painted natives. They reached the mouth of a huge river thirty miles wide, whose swift and powerful current struck the sea with such force that it lifted the ships anchored there by more than forty feet. The river was called *Marañon* by the natives; but Yañez baptized it *Río de Santa María de la Mar Dulce*. Later the Spaniards changed the name to *Amazonas*, because of rumors that tribes of warrior women lived on its banks. Yañez and his men learned from the Indians that the entire region was known as *Marinatambal,* the land to the east of the river being called *Canomora,* and that to the west *Paricora.* The natives were friendly and approached the Europeans without fear or apprehension. Unfortunately for them, they had no gold or pearls to trade, and their land, though fertile, did not produce anything worth taking. To make up for these deficiencies, the Spaniards captured 36 of these innocent and unsuspecting creatures to sell them in Spain as slaves. Las Casas severely condemned such criminal proceedings, which violated the letter and spirit of the capitulation.

After leaving the Marañon, they sailed almost straight north toward the Guyanas, and Polaris reappeared in their sky, for they had crossed the equator again. They proceeded northwest as far as Paria. Before reaching Trinidad, they found the delta of another huge river (the Orinoco). They called it *Rio Dulce,* because there also the powerful freshwater outflow kept rushing for miles into the sea before merging with it. They also named *Cabo de San Vicente* a headland on the Orinoco delta known today as Punta Pescador, because they wished to honor their leader, or because it was that saint's day (4 April). When they entered the *Boca de la Sierpe,* between Trinidad and the mainland, they noticed the strong current as Columbus had done 18 months before. On Paria and the surrounding islands, they found a great quantity of brazilwood, axed down many trees, and loaded 3,000 pounds of it, in direct violation of another clause in the capitulation, which prohibited the importation of brazilwood.

By reaching Paria and joining with the lands already discovered by the Hojeda and Niño–Guerra expeditions (Cumana, Maracapana, Curiana, Cauchieta and Coquibacoa), Yañez Pinzón demonstrated that from Cabo de São Roque to Cabo de la Vela there was a continuous coastline. Yañez thought that he had reached South Asia and was on the coast of India, not far from the Ganges. When Columbus had discovered Paria in August 1498, he too had asserted that it was a part of Asia, and this geographical misconception was pictured on maps and globes up to 1530. Pietro Martire agreed that such extensive coastline, from Cape Consolation to Cabo de la Vela and beyond, must belong to a continent and connect with Asia.[7]

In the islands they visited, the Spaniards found the villages deserted or destroyed, and the inhabitants taking refuge in forests or in mountain crags as soon as they saw the ships, perhaps because they had been the victims of frequent raids by cannibals; Las Casas insinuates, however, that they were probably hiding from the Christians, since Hojeda, La Cosa, and Cristóbal Guerra had been there. In the woods, Yañez and his men found trees producing the *cinnamon bark,* which like the real cinnamon was used to cure fever and headaches. They also found other trees so large that it took at least 16 men to encompass them with their arms.

Dwelling in those trees they noticed strange animals, which had the muzzle of a fox, the tail of a marmoset, the ears of a bat, the hands of a man, and the hind legs of a monkey. On their bellies they had a pouch, in which they nursed and carried their young. The animals in question were opossums.

After leaving Paria, Yañez sailed to the northeast and discovered an island that he named *Isla de Mayo* or May Island (probably Grenada). Then he went to Guadalupe, the Virgin Islands, and Puerto Rico. On 23 June he made port at Samaná, on the east coast of Hispaniola. Columbus recorded his arrival in one of his letters, but added that, unlike Hojeda, Yañez gave him little trouble.[8]

After leaving Hispaniola, Yañez sailed northwestward toward the Bahamas and reached Crooked Island Passage; but when the armada was anchored near the Baburca shoals, it was struck by a hurricane with such fury that two of the four ships sank right on the spot. Another broke loose from its moorings, drove off under the gale, and disappeared. The fourth held fast, but was so battered that it looked like a wreck. Afraid that it might sink any time, its crew deserted it and made for shore. Despairing for their lives, the stranded sailors thought of slaughtering the Indians who lived nearby, to keep them from warning the other villages and planning a general attack against the Christians. "But the Good and Merciful Lord forestalled such iniquity from being committed"; for the ship that had vanished with 18 men returned, and the one that was still anchored rode the storm and did not sink (July 1500).[9]

With these two remaining vessels, the expedition managed to return to Palos on 29 September. Its arrival brought sorrow to many homes, for in addition to the men who had been killed by the Indians, two of the four ships had sunk with most hands on board. The survivors had almost nothing to show for their ten months' voyage, except some stones that looked like topaz and a cargo of brazilwood. No wonder the investors, creditors, and bondsmen were alarmed and obtained a court order confiscating anything that might be turned into cash, and seizing the personal property of Yañez and his nephews. The latter complained to the Crown, alleging that before sailing they had bought on credit a considerable amount of supplies, and now the merchants wanted to be paid back at outlandish prices, from 50 to 100 per cent more than the merchandise was really worth. The Catholic Sovereigns wrote to the Town Council and to the judges of Palos, forbidding any expropriation of property until the Pinzóns had sold the 350 quintals of brazilwood they had brought back (5 December 1500), to give them a chance to pay back their debts with the product of that sale.[10] Yet six months later, his creditors were still pressing Vicente Yañez. Moreover, the crew members owed him 100,000 maravedis he had loaned them, which they were unable to pay him back, since they had gained nothing of value during the voyage and had no personal fortune. On 21 June 1501, the Crown agreed to take over the debts of these poor people and compensate Yañez with a like amount, thus providing him with funds to settle his own obligations.[11]

In spite of the financial failure of the expedition, Yañez's reputation as a navigator did not suffer. After all, he had been the first Spanish leader to cross the equator, and he had explored 600 leagues of coastline from Cape São Roque to Paria. In official circles, it was thought that this cape was within the sphere attributed to Spain by the Treaty of Tordesillas (1494), while later expeditions and astronomic calculations proved otherwise. For a number of years, there was disagreement between Spain and Portugal as to the exact location of the partition line, until it was agreed to set it vertically from the mouth of the Amazon to Cananea, a small island on the southeast coast of Brazil, not far from São Paulo (25° S.), leaving Cape São Roque under Portuguese jurisdiction. This was not known, however, when Vicente Yañez was granted another license to discover on 5 September 1501. He was named governor and captain-general of the coast from Cape Consolation to Cape San Vicente, including *Marinatambal* (Delta of the Amazon), and the *Río de Santa Maria de la Mar Dulce*.[12]

The usual clause about the payment of the Queen's *quinto* was included in the new capitulation. On the other hand, if the rulers of Spain decided to send one of their own vessels to barter on Yañez's coast, they would have to pay him one sixth of their profits. The prohibition to import slaves was maintained; but since no mention was made of brazilwood, it seems that Vicente would be allowed to bring back some and sell it in Spain. Yañez could outfit four ships. In each of them there was to be a chest or safe where all gold, pearls, and precious stones would be kept; and to watch over each safe and keep a record of its contents, there would be a comptroller appointed by the Crown. To make it easier for him to obtain the necessary supplies, Yañez was granted a *carta de saca de pan,* an authorization to take 7,200 bushels of bread out of the country (15 October 1501).[13] Because shortages were fairly frequent even in fertile Andalusia, no bread or flour could be exported without a special permit.

After that, we have no more records of Yañez Pinzón's second expedition. It does not seem to have sailed, since no mention of it is made in any document. Possibly it was called off, because as a result of his first failure, Yañez could not get sufficient financial backing; or because Portugal had just taken possession of the east coast of Brazil, through Alvares Cabral's landing at Porto Seguro.

Yet this aborted expedition was not a total loss, for its ships and men seem to have been retained by the Crown, to form part of the huge armada which in the spring of 1502 escorted the new governor of Hispaniola, Nicolas de Ovando, to Santo Domingo. There several of Yañez Pinzón's old companions met Bastidas and La Cosa, who had returned from the coast of Colombia with a sizable cargo of gold. This we know from later testimonies in the *Pleitos.*[14] Yañez did not leave Spain, and he spent the fall and winter months 1502–1503 in Seville, where he saw Bastidas and La Cosa render accounts and hand over their gold to the officials of the newly created House of Trade.[15]

4   Diego de Lepe
      1499–1500

"After Vicente Yañez, another discoverer, or rather destructor, came out in that same month of December 1499." Thus Las Casas begins his very succinct account of Diego de Lepe's voyage, which is largely derived from testimonies in the *Pleitos*.[1] Lepe was a native of Palos and a relative of Yañez Pinzón.[2] He does not seem to have taken part in any of Columbus' voyages; but a *criado* (servant) of his, called Miguel de Soria, sailed on the Niña as a *grumete* (apprentice seaman). Soria received four months' advance pay in Palos on 23 June 1492. Lepe vouched for him.[3]

Lepe, with two ships, left Spain about two weeks after Vicente Yañez, according to the majority of historians, or two weeks before, or at about the same time according to others. Possibly he and Yañez had been granted almost identical capitulations and had been expected to sail together. From the scant information we derive from Las Casas and the *Pleitos,* Lepe's voyage was almost a duplication of Yañez Pinzón's, except that Lepe struck land and took possession at a different place, which he called *Bay* or *River of San Julian* probably because it was that saint's day (12 February).[4] Like Yañez, he had fights with the Indians who killed 11 of his men when he entered the Amazon and sailed upstream for 70 leagues. Like Yañez, he kidnapped and brought back natives to Spain. According to Las Casas, he handed over his captives to Fonseca; and the Dominican upraided the bishop for his indifference toward Indian slavery, and for not punishing Lepe and other offenders who captured natives in violation of their capitulations.[5]

Like Vicente Yañez, Lepe explored the north coast of South America from the Brazilian elbow to the Orinoco delta: but he accomplished one thing the former had not done: he rounded Cape Santo Agostinho (8° 30′ S.) and sailed a few leagues south of it, thus being the first Spaniard to catch a glimpse of the east coast of Brazil. He did not proceed very far, however, but turned around and sailed west-north-west, toward the Amazon and Paria, as Yañez had done. It was not until the fall and winter months of 1500–1501 that the east coast of Brazil was really explored by Vélez de Mendoza and Luis Guerra.

When did Lepe return to Spain? We have no record of it. Just because he seems to have left two weeks after Yañez, it has been assumed that he returned some two weeks later. Yet we have grounds to believe that his voyage was much shorter and took less time. It is true that at the outset, he lost a few days rounding Cape Santo Agostinho and viewing the coast south of it. But from Paria, he seems to have sailed straight home while Pinzón explored the Windward and

Leeward Islands, stopped over in Hispaniola, was struck by a hurricane and lost two ships in Crooked Island Passage, which must have added up to a considerable delay. Therefore, it would not be wrong to infer that Lepe returned to Spain before Yañez, that is, before 29 September 1500.

The solution to this problem hinges on the whereabouts of the pilot Bartolomé Roldán in 1500, for during that year, according to various sources, he is credited with having taken part in three different expeditions: Hojeda–La Cosa, Lepe, and Vélez de Mendoza–Luis Guerra. There is no doubt that Bartolomé Roldán was much in demand as a pilot. As one of the witnesses in the *Pleitos* put it, "he [Roldán] has gone every time an armada has been sent there." Still it was physically impossible for him to do so, and his activities throughout the year 1500 require some checking.

We have already seen that Bartolomé Roldán did not take part in the Hojeda–La Cosa expedition of 1499–1500. On the other hand, we have Bartolomé's own testimony that he served under Diego de Lepe, and other crew members of Lepe's armada, testifying in the *Pleitos,* confirmed that he had sailed with them.[6] Now, if we consider the Vélez–Guerra expedition, we have positive proof that Bartolomé Roldán took part in it. The armada returned to Spain before 9 June 1501; and on 1 July Bartolomé Roldán, pilot of Vélez de Mendoza's caravel, empowered Antón García, pilot of Luis Guerra's caravel, to collect in his name any sums due him in salaries and in dividends resulting from the sale of Indian slaves and other things they had brought from America.[7] Therefore, Roldán served first with Lepe, and then with Vélez, and Lepe must have returned to Spain before Vélez sailed away. The latter was still in Seville on 18 August 1500; but he must have left before the end of the month, since according to sources, his voyage lasted ten months, and he was back before 9 June 1501. Lepe probably returned from his voyage in July 1500 or very early in August. In his report to Fonseca, he must have mentioned Cape Santo Agostinho and the coast running south of it; and this probably induced the bishop to send Vélez and Guerra sailing down that coast. On 18 August a new clause was introduced in Vélez's capitulation, ordering him to have his maps checked and to follow the route that would be traced for him.[8] This route led him to the east coast of Brazil south of Cape Santo Agostinho. And what better guide could he have than

Bartolomé Roldán, an experienced pilot who had just returned with Lepe from that cape?

In addition to Roldán, the following participants in Lepe's voyage are mentioned in the *Pleitos*: Juan Rodríguez de Mafra (he was also an investor), Juan Rodríguez (Lepe's brother), Pero Sánchez del Castillo, Martín de Arcos, Hernando Esteban, Juan González Portugués, Gonzalo de Vedya, Andrés García Valdín, Bartolomé García Ginovés, Cristóbal García, Luis del Valle, García de la Monja, and Alonso Rodríguez de la Calva.

After his return, Lepe had the same problems that plagued Yáñez Pinzón. His creditors harassed him, claiming higher sums than those agreed on before he sailed, because of an inflation in the price of food and supplies. Lepe begged the Crown to intervene in his favor, alleging that his creditors had "powerful relatives and friends," which made it impossible for him to be dealt with impartially. On 9 November 1500 the Catholic Sovereigns ordered the judicial authorities of Palos to see to it that the navigator was given a fair treatment.[9]

Lepe wanted to go back on another voyage of discovery, and on 15 November 1500 he secured from Fernando and Isabel the customary letter to Fonseca, asking the bishop to grant him an authorization to sail with three ships; but it took him ten months to obtain sufficient backing from investors, for he did not receive his capitulation until 14 September 1501.[10] According to this document, he could outfit four ships (instead of the three originally granted to him), and he could sail in them to the lands he had discovered earlier "to see more of them"; but he was forbidden to go to the lands already discovered by Columbus or any other person, and "to the islands and lands belonging to the Most Serene King of Portugal, our dearly beloved son. . . ." Where was he allowed to go, according to the terms of his capitulation? It could not be the north coast of Brazil, from Cape São Roque to the Orinoco, since this territory had been granted nine days earlier to Vicente Yáñez Pinzón. It must have been the east coast of Brazil, for Lepe had discovered Cape Santo Agostinho and had viewed the coast south of it, but without venturing to sail along it except for a few leagues. To be sure, this shore had just been explored by Vélez de Mendoza and Luis Guerra; but they had quarreled and shown no inclination to return there, so that it could be considered any man's land.

As an inducement to explore as much *new* coast as possible, Lepe was to hand over to the royal treasury only one sixth of the loot obtained in lands he would discover; but for anything of value acquired in regions he had already explored, he would have to pay as much as 50 per cent. No slaves were to be brought back; but he was allowed two quintals of brazilwood. There was the usual provisions for *escrivanos* (clerks), and on 16 October, the Crown ordered Gómez de Cervantes to appoint one for each of Lepe's ships.[11]

The armada was to sail before 1 November, but could not make it, and Lepe was granted a prolongation through 23 December.[12] During the month of November, he must have been very busy. On the 13th, he borrowed from the bookseller Juan de Camusa the sum of 6,200 maravedis, promising to account for it twenty days after his return. On 18 November he received from two investors, Alfonso Rodríguez, *trapero* (draper) of Seville, and Alonso de Villafranca, merchant of Valladolid, 10,000 mrs, pledging his word that he would render accounts two weeks after he reached Seville.[13] Then on 28 November, a meeting of the *compañía* was held. Lepe presided over it together with his second-in-command, Diego Rodríguez de la Mesquita, son of a wealthy shipowner of Triana.

From the minutes of this meeting ,which have never been published, we learn that the expedition was to consist of five ships: *Sant Spiritu, Santana, Castilla, Santa Ynes,* and a fifth vessel the name of which is not given but that belonged to Antón Benítez, a resident of the Puerto de Santa Maria. The investors present were Diego Ximenes the Younger, the draper Pedro Ruys, Alonso de Valladolid, Fernando de Carvajal, Gonzalo de Urea, Diego de Cervera, Diego Camacho, and (blank) de Ribera, all of them residents of Seville. Diego de Lepe, as captain general of the armada, pledged that he would render an account to each of them. All the sums invested were to be pooled together, and after the deduction of the costs, of the Crown's share, and of Lepe's bonus, the benefits would be divided into three parts in the usual manner: one third for the investors, one third for the shipowners, and one third for the crews. The captain general and the captains of the five vessels took an engagement not to make any stopovers on the way back, and to land only at Cadiz or Seville, where all the merchandise would be delivered intact and each investor would be paid his share. Any violation of this agreement would result in a fine of 1,000 gold *castellanos*.[14]

The meeting of the investors was usually held a few days before the departure of the fleet; but at the end of the year, Lepe was still in Seville. There had been a disagreement about the number of ships. Five had been freighted and outfitted, while the government maintained that Lepe should not exceed the four allotted to him in the capitulation (17 November). Later, however, the Catholic Sovereigns gave him permission to add the extra vessel (17 January 1502).[15]

Then, after this last date, nothing more is known of Lepe's second expedition. According to one testimony given in the *Pleitos,* Lepe went to Lisbon and died there shortly after.[16] Why did he go to Lisbon? Possibly because the King of Portugal had heard of his project and had voiced his strong disapproval, since the coast which Lepe was going to explore fell within the sphere granted to Portugal by the treaty of Tordesillas. The navigator may have gone to Lisbon to check the exact position of the demarcation line, and to allay the fears and suspicions of the Lusitanian monarch. There he could have become ill, or he could have been disposed of quietly as a troublemaker. He may well have been the victim of foul play for reasons of state. After his death, his vessels probably helped transport the troops and supplies that Nicolas de Ovando was taking to Santo Domingo.

In addition to Yáñez Pinzón's and Lepe's projected voyages, a third expedition was planned at about the same time, in the autumn of 1501 and, like the other two, it failed to materialize, probably for the same reason: Portuguese objections to Spanish intrusion in lands King Manoel considered his own. Juan de Escalante, a 21-year-old mariner who had accompanied Columbus on his third voyage (1498) and had been with him when Paria was discovered, was granted a capitulation on 5 October 1501.[17] The terms of this document are so vague that we don't know where he was planning to go. He was denied access to the lands belonging to the King of Portugal or already discovered. This means that he was excluded from all the territory between Cabo de Santo Agostinho and Cabo de la Vela. What he probably had in mind was the east coast of Brazil, not being aware that it was on the wrong side of the partition line and therefore off limits to Spaniards.

According to other clauses in his capitulation, Escalante was to sail with three ships. He could not bring back slaves, but was allowed one quintal of brazilwood. As for the royal treasury's share, Fernando and Isabel required only one sixth of the net profits, a fine display of generosity.

On 2 December 1501, Gonzalo Gómez de Cervantes was sent the usual order to appoint the *escrivanos* who were to serve on Escalante's ships.[18] Then we lose track of the youthful navigator until 18 February 1515, when he testified in the *Pleitos*.[19] He was then 35 years old and a resident of Cuba. In his testimony, he made no reference to his aborted voyage of discovery, which was probably canceled because of Portuguese objections.

Since we have been discussing projected expeditions that did not materialize, let us add another, even though its originator was not a Spaniard but Portuguese. In the royal letter, the name appears as Juan Dornelos or Dorvelos; but the man to whom it was addressed must have been Juan d'Ornelas, a resident of Terceira Island, one of the Azores. In those days, Terceira was the scene of considerable maritime activity, since several of its settlers (Pedro de Barcelos, Juan Fernandes Labrador, Gaspar Cortereal, etc.) were engaged in voyages of discovery across the North Atlantic, urged on by their monarch King Manoel the Fortunate. Manoel was fortunate indeed in having in his service faithful and enterprising subjects, who in the space of 20 years built him a huge colonial empire; but he was less fortunate in his dealings with them, for instead of rewarding their initiative, courage, skill and tenacity, he preferred the passive servility of his courtiers. It should be no surprise that men like Magellan, Esteban Gómez, Diogo Ribeiro, and the brothers Faleiro, tired of being ill-paid and ill-treated, shifted their allegiance and entered the service of Spain. Juan d'Ornelas was trying just that as early as 1500. He had been involved in disputes over distributions of lands in *Quatro Ribeiras,* the northern section of Terceira, and he was threatened with the loss of his estate. He contacted Fernando and Isabel, offering to go for them on a voyage of discovery. They answered on 6 May 1500 that he should come in person to the Court, or send someone duly authorized by him, to negotiate with the Spanish authorities; but we have no evidence that anything ever came out of that proposal.[20]

The Niño–Guerra expedition had been a financial success. Soon after its return a number of hardy souls tried to secure permission to sail to the shores of the new continent, hoping to make a fortune through pearl hunting. Since the Court had moved to Seville, residents of that city had the best chance of making themselves heard. Thus Rodrigo de Bastidas, a mariner of Triana, and Alonso Vélez de Mendoza, an hidalgo who divided his time between Moguer and Seville, were granted capitulations on 5 June 1500;[1] but Bastidas did not sail until the following year. Vélez Mendoza was the first to leave.

A man of noble birth, Vélez de Mendoza was *comendador* of the prestigious order of Santiago. His family probably originated in Jaen, where we find members of it in the fifteenth, sixteenth, and seventeenth centuries. Another Alonso Vélez de Mendoza was *contador* (treasurer) of the Queen's Household in 1501. The *comendador* must have been related to him, and his family connections probably played no small part in securing his capitulation; but although a member of an illustrious family, he had no personal fortune, and his commandery must have brought him only a small income. He had no home of his own. In Moguer he stayed with his brother-in-law Diego Quintero; in Seville, he lived in inns, but moved out when he could not pay his bills. On 22 February 1497, he acknowledged owing 30 silver *reales* to Juan Gómez de Zamora, a *mesonero* (innkeeper) of Alcalá de Guadaira, for meals and lodging.[2] On 8 February 1500, he borrowed 4,500 maravedis from his brother-in-law, 3,100 of which were to reimburse Catalina Ferrández, who seems to have been a *mesonera* of Seville.[3] On 21 April of the same year, wishing to recover a copy of Duns Scotus' *Sentences* which he had left in another lodging house, he had to appear before a notary and give power of attorney to a third party to reclaim his book.[4] His ownership of a philosophical work shows him to have been a man of culture, interested in intellectual speculations.

Perhaps there was some passage in the *Libri Sentenciarum* which had a special interest for him at that particular date, when he must have begun to plan for his voyage of discovery, and was about to submit his project to the rulers of Spain. If so, it may have been Duns Scotus' comment on the Earthly Paradise: "I say it is a place fit for human living. It should not be at a high altitude, nor under the equator, but in a temperate zone. Nor is there any need of locating it in the East, but should it be there, it would be equally temperate."[5] Perhaps the *comendador* fancied he would reach the Earthly Paradise, as Columbus claimed he had done in 1498.

Since he was unable to provide the funds for his armada, Vélez de Mendoza was forced to look for financial backing among the merchants of Seville. As early as 8 May, four weeks before he was granted his capitulation, he was already hunting for people willing to associate with him. The first he contacted were the Guerra brothers Antón Mariño and Luis.

Luis Guerra, like his brother Antón, provided flour and hardtack for ships going to America. In the *Libros de Armada* for the year 1495, he is mentioned as a *bizcochero*, and so is his nephew Alonso de Monroy.[6] The latter's widowed mother Beatriz Guerra was also in the hardtack business. In 1493 she had applied for permission to build and operate, on her Triana property, an oven to be used for the baking of bizcocho. Considering there was a need for such ovens, and wishing to compensate the widow for services rendered by Luis de Monroy her late husband, the City Council granted her the permit. She was to pay an annual tax of 31 maravedis. In addition she was forbidden to sell or lease the oven to any nobleman, churchman, or religious congregation. She could sell it only to a lay commoner. Evidently the City did not want the oven to fall into the hands of some tax-exempt member of the privileged classes.[7]

Alonso de Monroy appears in several documents as Luis Guerra's business associate. Beside baking bizcocho, they and several others made bricks, and they owned ovens where the bricks were baked.[8] On 20 February 1495, acting for his uncle who was out of town, Monroy rented a vineyard in Triana. Luis Guerra was to pay an annual rent of 550 maravedis, and had to prune the vines once a year in the presence of expert viticultors.[9] We shall see later how Alonso de Monroy accompanied his uncles Luis and Cristóbal in their last voyage of discovery, in the course of which all three lost their lives.

Luis Guerra is also mentioned in other documents as a *cambiador* (banker); he also traded with *traperos* (drapers), from whom he bought large stocks of woven fabrics. Although they were mere bourgeois merchants, the Guerras enjoyed enough wealth and social consideration to contract matrimonial alliances with the petty nobility. Their father Diego had married into the Mariño family, and so had an aunt or a sister, Catalina Guerra, who in 1495 is referred to as the widow of Cristóbal Ferrandez Mariño. As for Luis himself, his wife Beatriz de Gallegos belonged to the local gentry. During the period which interests us, there was a Gallegos on the Seville City Council.

When Vélez de Mendoza approached Antón and Luis on 8 May, he showed them the preliminary letter he had obtained from the Catholic Sovereigns, which allowed him to sail with four ships. Both brothers promised to provide jointly and at their own cost a caravel, and to have it fitted out before the end of June. They were to keep their own gains except for the King's share; but they would acknowledge Vélez as the leader of the expedition. In exchange, the latter agreed to equip another ship. If he could not do so before the appointed time (30 June), or if he gave up his project, the Guerras were free to sail without him. This means that the capitulation he hoped to get from Fonseca would be transferable to Antón and Luis in case he did not sail; and even if he went with them, except for recognizing him as *capitán general,* they would have considerable freedom of action. Vespucci must have had a similar arrangement with Hojeda. Another interesting clause was included in the agreement between Vélez and the Guerra brothers: the *comendador* renounced his special status as member of a military order and put himself under the jurisdiction of the authorities of Seville.[10] He was to regret it later.

During the next few days, Luis Guerra put his affairs in order. On 13 May he acknowledged that he owed his wife Beatriz de Gallegos 70,000 maravedis. This was the amount he had received from her parents fifteen years before as her dowry. He also set aside for her 500 silver *doblas* (35,500 maravedis) of his money, making it possible for her to claim both sums whenever she wished to do so. On the same day he also gave Beatriz two powers of attorney, authorizing her to run his business and to represent him in court during his absence.[11]

Meanwhile, Vélez was trying to find more vessels. On 9 May he took an option on a caravel called the *San Pedro.* Vélez was to pay 9,000 maravedis a month to the master Alonso García de Villalba for the freighting of the ship, which was to be outfitted no later than 15 June, so that the loading of supplies and merchandise could start immediately after that date. Unfortunately, García de Villalba was only half-owner of the *San Pedro;* if his partner did not agree, the deal would fall through. Apparently this is what happened, for Vélez sailed without the *San Pedro.*[12]

As the comendador needed cash to buy supplies, he borrowed 15,000 maravedis from Carlos de Hontiveros, who had sailed with Columbus on his third voyage. On 27 May Vélez borrowed an additional 10,000 maravedis from Pedro Maldonado.[13] As he negotiated with Fonseca, he still hoped to sail with four ships, since he had been allowed that many by the Catholic Sovereigns. The capitulation he obtained from the bishop on 5 June confirmed that number; but either because no other vessels were available, or because he lacked the necessary funds, he had to be satisfied with two caravels.

The one outfitted by the Guerras, the *Sant* (or *Santi*) *Spiritu* belonged to Luis Rodríguez de la Mesquita, a resident of Triana who deserves special mention. He was a *comitre,* and he served at least one term as *alcalde* (administrator) of the Brotherhood. We have seen already that a *comitre* was a sort of naval reserve officer who served with his ship whenever he was called to duty. In addition to his naval activities as a *comitre* and a shipowner, Luis de la Mesquita had been in charge of the Triana bridge for twelve years. It was a floating wooden structure, whose floor rested on boats anchored in the river and held together by cables. It was in need of constant repair. For his work, Luis received 225,000 maravedis a year.[14] Also, at various times, being the highest bidder at public auctions, he was awarded the task of collecting taxes in Triana and in towns placed under Seville's jurisdiction. He cut quite a figure in Triana and was a respected member of his community. He and his wife gave the Santa Ana church the baptismal font that is still used today, and on which the following inscription can be read; "This font was laid on the eve of Our Lady Santa Ana, the year of the Lord 1499. It was the gift of Luis Rodríguez de la Mesquita and Elvira González de Vallejo his wife."[15] We have already mentioned that one of Luis's sons, Diego de la Mesquita, was chosen by Diego de Lepe to be his second in command for his projected voyage, which was canceled.

According to the terms of their contract with the *comendador,* one of the Guerra brothers was to take part in the expedition; but finally both brothers sailed on the *Sant Spiritu*, Luis as captain and Antón as *escrivano* (clerk). Other members of the crew were as follows: master, Juan Rodríguez de la Lanza, an old-time associate of Luis de la Mesquita; *contramaestre* (mate), Luis López; pilots, the comitre, Bartolomé Diaz, and Antón García. The latter, a native of Triana, was the brother of the Alonso García who had been a participant in Columbus' third voyage and had served as pilot on the Peralonso Niño–Cristóbal Guerra caravel. We also find on the *Sant Spiritu* Cristóbal de Vergara, Alonso de Jaen, and Juan Gallego, officially listed as *marineros;* but they really seem to have been financial backers who enlisted as seamen to better protect their share of the investment. To help outfit the *Sant Spiritu,* Luis Guerra and Juan de la Lanza borrowed 15,600 maravedis from Gonzalo Ferrández, and 3,400 more from Ruy González de la Sal, both merchants of Seville, on 8 August 1500.[16]

The owner of the other caravel, the *Sant Cristóbal,* was Pedro Ramírez. His brother Alvaro and the latter's father-in-law, an apothecary named Antonio, also put out money in this venture. The pilot was Bartolomé Roldán who had just returned to Spain with Diego de Lepe. The *escrivano* was Juan de Chaves, and the master Cristóbal Rodríguez Tiscareño. The latter belonged to a family of *comitres* who made frequent voyages to the New World. To help outfit his ship, Tiscareño had borrowed 14,000 maravedis from his mother.[17] Naturally, Vélez de Mendoza commanded the *Sant Cristóbal.*

We have seen that the comendador and Rodrigo de Bastidas had been granted their capitulations on the same day (5 June) and in practically the same terms, the main difference being that Vélez could outfit four ships, while Bastidas was allowed only two. Both could go anywhere in the Indies, except to the lands previously discovered by Columbus nad Cristóbal Guerra. They were to return to Cadiz and report to Ximeno de Briviesca, to whom they were to hand over the *cuarto* (fourth) of the profits after deduction of the costs. This was a rather stiff payment, for Vicent Yañez Pinzón had been required to pay only one fifth.

It so happened that after these permits were issued, Alonso de Hojeda returned from his voyage (about 15 June), and this caused some modifications in the capitulations. On 20 July Pedro Ramírez and Cristóbal Tiscareño, owner and master of the *Sant Cristóbal,* were

summoned before Fonseca with other investors and were read a modified version, in which Hojeda's land was declared taboo, and his name
added to those of Columbus and Cristóbal Guerra. The following day,
it was the turn of another financial backer, Alonso de Cordoba, *trapero*
(cloth merchant) of Baeza; and two days later (22 July), Alonso
Vélez himself appeared before Fonseca and pledged his property,
personal and real, that he would keep the terms of the modified capitulation. On 18 August Vélez de Mendoza and Pedro Ramírez were
summoned again before the notary Fernando Ruiz de Porras, who read
to them a third draft of a portion of the capitulation. In it, the land
discovered by Hojeda was mentioned by name as "the islands of
Arquibacoa," and Vélez and his men were strictly forbidden to go
anywhere near it, because of some "secret" which the Court did not
want to be known. The "secret" in question was the fact that Hojeda
had discovered precious stones in Coquibacoa. Two new clauses, which
did not appear in the original capitulation, were read to Vélez de
Mendoza on that day: (1) no foreigner was to be allowed on his ships;
(2) he should have his sailing charts checked, and he should follow
the route that would be traced for him.[18]

These two additional clauses are worthy of note, for the first was
probably meant to keep Vespucci out, and the second resulted from
Diego de Lepe's return, which must have taken place in late July or
early August 1500. We have positive proof that Lepe was back in
Spain before Vélez sailed, since one of Lepe's pilots Bartolomé Roldán
joined the Vélez–Guerra expedition, as pilot of the *Sant Cristóbal,* the
comendador's caravel. On his return, Lepe had reported the discovery
of Cape Santo Agostinho, and this may have given Fonseca the idea of
sending Vélez south of that cape, to explore the hitherto unknown
coastline beyond, under the expert guidance of Bartolomé Roldán.

Very likely Luis Guerra, Antón Mariño and their backers similarly
had to swear that they would observe the terms of the revised capitulation, although we have no documentary record of it.

The expedition sailed shortly after 18 August 1500. Since it
returned before 9 June 1501, the voyage must have lasted slightly less
than the ten months mentioned in some documents. What route did
it follow and where did it go? There is no doubt that the land explored was part of the coast of Brazil south of Cape Santo Agostinho
(8° 30′ S.). This we infer from testimonies given in the *Pleitos de*

Colón in 1512–1513 by four experienced pilots, each of whom had taken part in one or several of the Andalusian voyages: Andrés de Morales, Antón García, Juan de Xerez, and Arias Pérez Pinzón. The question put to them was the following: "Do you know that Diego de Lepe and those who went with him . . . discovered from the said cape (Santa Cruz or Santo Agostinho) the coast that runs down south, to a point where it is now discovered."

To this question, the pilot André de Morales answered that "Diego de Lepe discovered a small section of that coast, and later one called Alonso Vélez discovered from Cape Cruz toward the south all that is discovered now." Antón García testified that "he and Luis Guerra and Alonso Vélez who went with him discovered the region referred to in the question, while Diego de Lepe and Vicente Yañez remained behind on the north coast. He knows this because he saw it, and this witness does not believe that the Admiral nor anyone else had been there before, because the Indians did not remember having seen Christians, and they marveled at what they saw." Antón García had been pilot of the *Sant Spiritu,* Luis Guerra's caravel. This gives specail value to his testimony. Answering the same question, the pilot Juan de Xérez declared that "he and those who went in his company with Vicente Yañez, discovered from Cape Santa Cruz to Paria following the coast, and later, four or five months after he sailed away, Alonso Vélez and Luis Guerra left Seville, and went to discover the region referred to in the question, and from Cape Santa Cruz they discovered the southern coast as far as it has been discovered now, and that before or after neither the Admiral nor anyone else had been there, since no mention of it could be found on any sailing chart."

In 1515 more witnesses were questioned in Andalusia. On 9 October, in Palos, Arias Pérez, who had accompanied his uncle Vicente Yañez Pinzón in the 1499–1500 voyage gave the following testimony: "The comendador Francisco [sic] Vélez, a resident of Moguer, discovered that [land] at the time that this witness had returned from his voyage of discovery, and through the information he gave them, Vélez [and his companions] went ahead, rounded Cape Santo Agostinho, sailed southward and discovered the coast. . . . Asked how he knows it, this witness said that Francisco Vélez informed him and gave him an account of his discovery . . . and showed him the land pictured on a map he had made." The above testimony implies that

Vicente Yañez Pinzón had returned before Vélez and Guerra sailed; but this is unlikely since Yañez did not reach Spain until one month later, on 29 September 1500.[19]

Even more significant is the declaration made on a different occasion by another participant in the voyage. In 1515, when Spaniards and Portuguese were quarreling about the boundaries of their respective possessions in South America, the officials of the House of Trade in Seville ordered an inquiry to determine the exact position of Cape Santo Agostinho. A pilot named Juan Rodríguez Serrano testified that he did not know it, because when he had been with Vélez de Mendoza, he was only an adolescent and had not yet learned how to take the height of the sun; but he remembered this much about the voyage: they had sailed from Seville in two caravels under the command of Vélez de Mendoza, had first gone to the Canaries, and then to Santiago, one of the islands in the Cabo Verde archipelago. After sailing a number of leagues from Santiago, they ran into bad weather and were driven south-southwest until they sighted land five or six leagues north of Cape Santo Agostinho. They rounded the cape without difficulty and kept sailing south-southwest until they turned back. He estimated the distance between the cape and Santiago at about 560 leagues.[20]

His testimony is corroborated by documents of the Archivo de Protocolos, from which we learn that both ships sailed from the Torre del Oro in Seville and made stopovers in Gran Canaria and Santiago Island. We also know that they reached the coast of Brazil, since two of the Indian captives who were brought to Seville and sold as slaves were said to be natives of a land called "Topia."[21] If the land in question was south of Cape Santo Agostinho, these Indians must have been Topaya or Tupi Indians, since these ethnic groups shared possession of the shores of the Bahia–Pernambuco region at the time of its discovery by the Europeans. The "Río de Cervatos" (Fawn or Deer River), at whose mouth the armada was anchored on Christmas Day, 1500, may have been the São Francisco River.[22] Thus Vélez de Mendoza's caravels seem to have been the first Spanish expedition to reach that part of Brazil. We must keep in mind that Alvares Cabral struck land in April 1500 at Porto Seguro, farther south, and took possession of the "Island of Santa Cruz" in the name of the King of Portugal;

but this was not yet known in Spain at the time Vélez and Luis Guerra sailed from Seville.

From other documents in the Archivo de Protocolos we learn that Vélez de Mendoza had returned to Spain before 9 June 1501, because on that day Cristóbal Tiscareño leased out the *Sant Cristóbal* to the Genoese merchant Jacome de Riberol. At the time this transaction was made, the *Sant Cristóbal* was anchored in the Puerto de las Muelas, in the Guadalquivir, opposite the Torre del Oro.[23]

Although both caravels returned in good shape to Spain, the voyage had been far from peaceful, for the two captains had quarreled, and their dispute had to be settled by judges after they reached Seville. The cause of the trouble was the partition of the profits. Before leaving Spain the captains, the shipowners, and the masters had reached an agreement. We are not told what it was, but it seems that each vessel would keep its own booty, and that each captain would divide it among his crew. This agreement was put into writing in Las Palmas de Gran Canaria, and was sworn to by all before a crucifix in a church of Santiago Island.

But when the expedition reached the coast of Brazil, Luis Guerra's men made a foray inland, met with stiff resistance, and several of them lost their lives. This unfortunate event had its positive side for the survivors, since it meant more room for booty, particularly for Indian captives, on the *Sant Spiritu,* Guerra's caravel, and bigger profits for each member of its crew. Alonso Vélez did not relish this development, nor did his master Cristóbal Tiscareño. They proposed a new partition, according to which all the gains would be pooled and divided among all the men, no matter which ship they belonged to. At first Luis Guerra refused; but since his men were outnumbered, and since Vélez and Tiscareño threatened to use force, he acceded to the terms proposed by them. A new agreement was made on Christmas Day, 1500, in the Río de Cervatos harbor, in the presence of the *escrivanos* Mariño and Chaves; Luis Guerra never intended to keep it, but he said nothing until they returned to Spain. In Cadiz, where they made port to report to Ximeno de Briviesca as the capitulation prescribed, Luis formally declared before a notary that he did not feel bound by the Río de Cervatos agreement.[24]

We have seen that the caravels reached Seville before 9 June 1501.

On 12 June Vélez de Mendoza empowered his brother-in-law Diego Quintero to undertake the partition of slaves and merchandise among the members of both crews.[25] On 16 June Cristóbal Tiscareño had a summons issued to Luis Guerra and his master Juan de la Lanza, enjoining them to keep the agreement made on 25 December at the Río de Cervatos; but both refused to do so.[26] Since no understanding could be reached, the matter was left for judges to decide. On 3 July Luis Guerra's men empowered him to represent them in court, and to avoid any hardship which the delay might cause them, he paid them off in full out of his own pocket.[27] Then, without waiting for the case to be decided in court, each side began selling its Indian captives.

On 7 July, Antón Mariño sold to Fernando de Toledo, merchant of Jerez, a seven-year-old boy and a twenty-year-old girl, each of whom was said to be a native of "Topia." The price agreed on for both was 7,000 maravedis.[28] Luis Guerra sold a girl named Sunbay for 6,000 maravedis to Alonso de Medina, a swordsmith; but a few days later the girl became so ill that it looked as if she would soon die, and the swordsmith asked for his money back. Naturally Guerra refused, alleging that the girl was in excellent health when he sold her, and that Alonso de Medina, far from being pressured into buying her, had had plenty of time to examine her, and had even taken her to his home to show her to his wife before concluding the sale.[29] In his reply to Medina's demand, Luis Guerra made a pertinent comment on "indios bozales," that being the name given to fresh captives who had not yet learned Spanish and were still untrained for any kind of work. This is what he wrote about them: "In the case of Bozal Indians who come from a distant land, they undergo so much change and such trials, that the vendor is not obligated and cannot be held responsible for anything that may affect the health and frame of mind of the slaves."

Vélez de Mendoza too had some American natives to sell. One of his employees, Rodrigo de Lepe, sold for 6,000 maravedis, to the tanner Pedro López de Gavilán, a 25-year-old Indian who became ill a few days later. The tanner asked for his money back but, it may be doubted that he got it, although he claimed that Rodrigo de Lepe had promised to return the money in case of serious illness.[30]

The sale of his Indians does not seem to have brought the *comendador* much profit, for he soon found himself in serious financial trouble. On 4 September he borrowed from Martín Navarro, an innkeeper, the sum of 2,516 maravedis;[31] but this was not enough to save him from his creditors, and on 1-October we find him in jail for debts. Martín Navarro again came to his rescue and made a deal with the jailer: Vélez would be unchained and allowed to move about freely in the prison building; if he escaped, Navarro would be held responsible and would have to pay Vélez' debts. On the other hand, Vélez empowered the innkeeper to represent him in court (probably in his lawsuit against Luis Guerra), and promised to split evently with him whatever money might be obtained from the settlement of the case, after deduction of the costs.[32]

Then on 29 October the comendador made a far-reaching agreement with the innkeeper. At that time Vélez was trying to obtain another capitulation from the Crown. He promised Navarro, "his loyal and true friend," half of whatever gain might be obtained from such a capitulation, and if the *comendador* were to lead another expedition of discovery, Navarro would command one of the ships. Meanwhile, the innkeeper was to keep him in funds and pay for all his expenses.[33]

Vélez did secure another capitulation (15 February 1502), but of a different character. He was authorized to found a new town in Hispaniola and to settle in it 50 families of Castilian immigrants.[34] Vélez and his colonists sailed from Spain in March 1503. Navarro did not go along, but shipped a cargo of merchandise. Unfortunately the *Libro de Armadas* which contains detailed information concerning the *comendador's* voyage to Hispaniola (AGI, Contratacíon 3250) was misplaced some thirty years ago and has not been found since. One of the last scholars to consult it, Father Angel Ortega, refers to it and quotes from it in his work on La Rábida.[35] Father Ortega confused our *comendador* with Alonso Vélez, *alcalde mayor* of Palos in 1532. This identification cannot be accepted, since our Alonso Vélez figures on a list of Sevillans who died in Santo Domingo before 1512.[36]

As for Luis Guerra, he seems to have fared better than Vélez de Mendoza as a result of the voyage they had made together. The judges may have decided the lawsuit in his favor, and being the shrewd merchant that he was, he probably understood commercial and legal affairs much better than the noble *comendador*. At any rate, instead of borrowing money as Vélez had done, we find him making a loan. On

16 January 1502, he lent 22,000 maravedis to Diego Rodríguez de Grajeda, to help him supply a caravel which was about to sail for Santo Domingo.[37] The year before, Diego de Grajeda had been on a voyage of discovery with Cristóbal, youngest of the Guerra brothers.

6   Cristóbal Guerra and Diego de Grajeda
1500–1501

When Luis Guerra and Antón Mariño returned to Spain in June 1501, their younger brother Cristóbal was absent, having left shortly after they did on another voyage of exploration. His first venture, made jointly with Peralonso Niño, had been such a financial success that the Queen had decided almost immediately to send him back to the "Costa de las Perlas"; but this new undertaking was very different from his previous voyage. Instead of being a purely commercial venture, backed by private capital for personal gain, it was a state enterprise financed almost entirely by the Crown, in which Cristóbal played the part of a government official responsible directly to the Queen and not to investors. We know this from the instructions sent on 28 June 1500, by the treasurer Alonso Morales to one of this subordinates Alonso Alvárez; the latter was to organize the expedition in cooperation with Juan de Fonseca and Ximeno de Briviesca, who were in charge of the affairs of the Indies in Seville and in Cadiz respectively.[1]

The expedition was to consist of two vessels, one of which at least was to be provided by the *comitre* Diego Rodríguez de Grajeda, who lived in Triana. In addition to being in the shipping business for himself and being the owner of various vessels, Grajeda carried out several official missions to Hispaniola for the Spanish government, and he appears in 1507 in a document as *maestre e capitan de la nao mayor de su Alteza, comitre*.[2] According to Morales' instructions, Grajeda's caravel, of about 100 tons, was to earn during the trip 110 maravedis per ton and per month. The other vessel, still to be found, was to be much smaller, of only 50 tons. Grajeda provided it as well. The composition of the crews, with their monthly salaries as stipulated, may be seen in the table.

	Grajeda's Caravel	Smaller Caravel	Monthly Salary (in maravedis)
Pilot (*piloto*)	1	1	1,500
Master (*maestre*)	1	1	1,500
Mate (*contramaestre*)	1	1	1,350
Able seamen (*marineros*)[a]	14	10	900
Apprentice seamen (*grumetes*)	10	7	600
Cabin boys (*pajes*)	3	3	300
Soldiers or guards (*hombres de armas*)	10	7	850
Total	40	30	

[a] On each ship there were to be included among the *marineros* a caulker, a carpenter and a cooper who would collect, in addition to their salary as sailors, 500 maravedis more, making a total of 1,400 a month for each.

There followed a detailed list of all the supplies required for both vessels. The total expenditure, including the leasing of the ships and three months' advance pay for both crews, amounted approximately to 425,000 maravedis, of which Grajeda was to pay one fifth (85,000). Cristóbal Guerra does not seem to have invested anything in this venture. Alonso Álvarez actually put all the above arrangements into effect, as is indicated in a note in red ink at the margin of his instructions, which runs as follows: "Alonso Álvarez did all what he had been told and rendered accounts to the treasurer." In these instructions, Grajeda is given the title of captain. He must have sailed on his own ship, with Cristóbal going on the smaller vessel of 50 tons, though retaining command of the expedition as a whole.[3]

The date of sailing seems to have been in the late summer or early fall of 1500. Of the participants in this voyage, besides Guerra and Grajeda, we know the names of only two: Pedro de la Puebla and Juan de Noya, respectively pilot and cooper of the smaller caravel.[4] Since this vessel seems to have returned alone, Alice B. Gould has expressed the opinion that the larger caravel was lost; but I don't think so, for on this ship was its owner and captain Diego de Grajeda. There is no doubt that the *comitre* personally took part in the expedition, since he said so himself in a notarial act dated 30 September 1502. He was then trying to collect 29,930 maravedis still owed him by the Crown "for the service he rendered with one of his caravels during the voyage in which he went to the Islands of the Indies and the Costa de las Perlas, the Captain of the said caravel being Cristóbal Guerra."[5] The 29,930 maravedis he was asking for were in partial payment for the freighting of the smaller caravel. We also know that Grajeda was in Seville on 11 March 1501, when he formed a company with the Genoese merchant Jacome de Riberol, for the construction at common expense of a caravel to be named *Santa Ana*.[6] When Grajeda made that deal, he must have been back from the Costa de las Perlas. I am under the impression that both vessels sailed together from Spain in the late summer of 1500, and that Guerra sent back Grajeda in the larger ship with a cargo of pearls and brazilwood at the beginning of the year 1501, while he himself tarried on the Costa de las Perlas and possibly stopped over in Hispaniola before going back to Spain.

As to the date of Cristóbal's return, Alice Gould gives 5 October 1501, since on that day a Spanish caravel arrived at Cadiz bringing 60 slaves, 300 quintals of brazilwood, and 50 marcs (25 pounds) of pearls of very uneven quality. This information is found in a letter addressed on 17 October to the duke of Ferrara by his agent in Lisbon, Alberto Cantino, who had seen some of those pearls that had been brought to Lisbon.[7] According to Cantino's letter, the vessel had returned from the *Islands of Antilla* (the West Indies), and no mention was made of the Costa de las Perlas. Yet it does not seem unreasonable to suppose that it was Guerra's 50-ton caravel, although we have no positive proof of it. At any rate, there is no doubt that Cristóbal was back before 1 November.

We know very little about this expedition since historians of the time ignored it or confused it with Cristóbal's other voyages. Juan de Noya gave an eyewitness account of it in the *Pleitos,* but it is very short and incomplete. After stopping over in Gran Canaria, the vessels reached the Costa de las Perlas. The Spaniards landed in Curiana, where they obtained pearls, brazilwood, and cassia fistula.[8] From Curiana, Cristóbal probably sent home Grajeda in the larger vessel. Apparently, he was not satisfied with his pickings, for the pearls he had found were small and not very clear; and he decided to assault Bonaire Island, which stands just north of Cape Tucacas. In spite of strict orders from the Queen not to molest the natives, Cristóbal and his men killed a number of Indians, captured many others, and loaded them on his caravel. Then they returned to Cadiz with their human cargo. Briviesca must have been out of town, for Cristóbal reported to the notary public Juan de Faya.

At the time the Court was in Ecija, not far from Seville, but the Queen did not learn the truth immediately. At first she merely ordered Cristóbal to render accounts to Ximeno de Briviesca, and to send him an Indian girl whom she had heard he had brought back (10 and 11 November).[9] By 1 December, however, she had found out that Cristóbal had been selling Indians in Cadiz, Jerez, Seville, and Cordoba. Becoming very indignant, she ordered Gonzalo Gómez de Cervantes to arrest Cristóbal and his accomplices, and to have the Indians freed and returned to their homeland at Cristóbal's expense. She also ordered a general inquiry, declaring that she wanted the culprits to be tried and properly punished. Here is a condensed version of her letter to Gómez de Cervantes.

"Gonzalo Gómez de Cervantes, our *corregidor* of the city of Jerez de la Frontera, we have been informed that Cristóbal Guerra—who by our command went to the lands of Cumana and Cuchina (Curiana) where pearls are found in the ocean—and others by his order captured and killed Indians of both sexes on the island of *Poynare* (Bonaire), and those they brought back alive they sold in the city of Seville, and in Cadiz, Jérez, Cordova and other parts, and some are still in their power; and since this was done against our command and prohibition, the said Indians being our subjects, we want to know exactly how this came to pass, and . . . by the present (letter) we order you to investigate and find the truth by any ways and means possible, how many Indians of both sexes Cristóbal Guerra and his companions brought back and sold, and to whom and at what price, and how many have been sold or are still in their power; . . . and if you find that all this is true, take immediately all the sums paid for such sales from Cristóbal Guerra, returning to each buyer the amount he has paid; and as for those who have not yet been sold, take them in your power, and hand them over to the Comendador de Lares (Ovando), our governor of the Islands and Tierra Firme of the Ocean Sea, that he may return them to the island from which they were taken, and set them free . . . And since we want to know exactly what happened, and how guilty are those who are responsible for it, send us complete information duly certified and sealed by a notary, that we may study this case and render proper justice. Meanwhile, we order you to keep Cristóbal Guerra and his accomplices in jail and under heavy guard, and release no one and grant no bail without our authorization . . ."[10]

There are other letters from the Queen on the same subject and in the same tone, dated 9 and 12 December. Why did Isabel act so sternly against Cristóbal, when a few months before she had not objected to Vélez de Mendoza and Luis Guerra selling their Indian captives? As a matter of fact, she was collecting her share on such transactions, and on 28 July 1503, she was even to complain that Luis Guerra and Pedro Ramírez had been lax in meeting tax payments on their slave sales.[11]

The answer to this apparent dilemma is obvious. The natives brought back by Vélez and Luis Guerra were from "Topia" (Brazil), a land that belonged to Portugal according to the treaty of Tordesillas. This had just become known in Spain through a letter from King Manoel of Portugal to Fernando and Isabel (summer 1501), informing them of Alvares Cabral's discovery of the Land of Santa Cruz. On the other hand, the Indians of Bonaire Island were subjects of the Catholic Sovereigns, and as such could not be enslaved. The matter is very clearly stated in Isabel's letter to Gonzalo Gómez de Cervantes: ". . . the said Indians being our subjects . . . (siendo los dichos indios nuestros súbditos)."

Apparently this was the official attitude of the Spanish Crown. We give another example of it. In 1525, when Esteban Gómez returned to Coruña from his vain attempt to find a northwest passage, he sold a number of Indians he had captured on the coast of Maine. They were set free on orders from the Court, for it was claimed that the whole coast of North America was Spanish territory. Two years later, however, the galleon *San Gabriel,* one of Loaysa's ships, reached Coruña with a load of Brazilian natives, subjects of the king of Portugal, who were sold publicly without any objection from the Spanish authorities. Doctor Beltrán, a member of the Council of the Indies, bought one of them.[12]

Of course, this rule did not apply to "cannibals" and other rebellious Indians who refused to submit to the Spaniards. If captured in war, they could be reduced to slavery. More will be said about this shortly in our discussion of the Guerras' last voyage.

Rodrigo de Bastidas received his license to sail on 5 June 1500, the same day as Vélez de Mendoza.[1] Both capitulations were couched in the same terms, except that Bastidas was limited to two ships, while Vélez had been allowed four. An error of Martín Fernández de Navarrete, who read on a document "escrivano de Sevilla" instead of "vecino de Sevilla," has led many historians to believe that Bastidas was a notary.[2] In early sixteenth century texts, he is usually referred to as a mariner or as a merchant, and he probably was both. He seems to have been a man of means, for he owned extensive property in Triana. He was married to Isabel Rodríguez de Romera.

Yet, however wealthy he may have been, he could not alone finance an expedition to the New World. So he organized a *compañía* of investors. Securing the collaboration of Juan de la Cosa no doubt opened many doors to him. Through the minutes of a stockholders' meeting that is undated but must have taken place shortly before sailing, we know the names of his backers and how much each of them invested in the enterprise. In all they were twenty, and they invested a total of 377,547 maravedis. Many of them were wealthy merchants (Juan de Ledesma, Diego de Haro, Alfonso Rodríguez, Luis de Negrón, Diego Hurtado, Diego Ximenes); and some put up money in two or more voyages. Others were men of high rank who occupied commanding positions in the city: the Duke of Medina Sidonia, *alcalde mayor* (chief justice), and the Count of Cifuentes, *asistente* (chief administrator). Others were local government officials: a *mayordomo* (treasurer of Seville), a *jurado* (justice of the peace), an *alguazil* (constable). They invested directly or through an aide or a relative. In some cases the money they laid out was their own in part only, the rest being provided by a friend or a business associate. Of the 35,000 which the draper Diego de Haro placed in the enterprise, 10,000 belonged to another draper, Pedro Ruys.

Here is the list of the financial backers of this expedition, with the sums that each invested in it.

maravedis

The *jurado* Pedro de Valladolid	25,000
Alfonso Rodríguez, *trapero* (draper)	50,000
Alfonso de Villafranca ⎱ Bartolomé de Carrión ⎰	25,000
Juan Velásquez, retainer of the Count of Cifuentes	5,000
Francisco Descobar	10,000
Luis de Negrón	14,000
García Pérez de Cabrera, son of the mayordomo of the City, Juan de Sevilla	40,000
Martín de Torres, barber	10,000
Diego Hurtado	22,000
Diego Maldonado	10,000
Rodrigo de Mexia, chamberlain of the duke of Medina Sidonia	15,237
Francisco de Zavallos, *alguazil*	14,010
Juan de Grado	13,500
Fernando de Sevilla	13,800
Diego Ximenes the Younger	20,000
Juan de Morales ⎱ Francisco de Zavallos the Younger ⎰	15,000
Juan de Ledesma	40,000
Diego de Haro, *trapero*	35,000

According to the agreement they made with Bastidas, the fleet was to consist of two vessels: the caravel *San Antón,* and the *nao* (cargo ship) *Santa María de Gracia,* escorted by a bergantin and a *chinchorro* (fishing boat). It was to sail within ten days. If before Bastidas returned to Spain, he sent back the *nao* with part of his gains, the cargo would have to be consigned to a committee of three, formed by Alfonso Rodríguez, Diego Ximenes, and a priest named Juan de Romera (a relative of Bastidas's wife). This committee would take stock of the merchandise and be responsible for it. When Bastidas himself returned, he should land in Andalusia and not anywhere else, and he could not sell or dispose of the merchandise for twenty days, until he had given full account of it to his backers.

The way the profits were to be divided made sure that the investors would get most of it. First, the King's share (one fourth of the net) would be set aside. Then a flat sum of 100,000 maravedis would be assigned to the investors. Finally, the rest was to be split into three equal parts: one for the shipowners, one for the crews, and the last for the investors.[3]

The ships probably came from the Bilbao shipyards, since both masters, Antonio de Escalante and Martín de Buniorte (or Buniol) were from Vizcaya. More than one third of the crew members listed on the payrolls had Basque names.[4] Escalante was accompanied by his son who served as seaman.

The two pilots were Juan de la Cosa—who had been promised a big bonus—and Gonzalo de Lorca. Andrés de Morales also took part in the expedition, but he does not seem to have served as a full-fledged pilot.

Both *veedores* (comptrollers) Juan de Ayala and Luis de Negrón had been appointed by Gonzalo Gómez de Cervantes. They were to watch over the gold, pearls, and precious stones, and protect the Queen's interests. In addition to being *veedor*, Negrón was also an investor; as such he may have been more intent on protecting his own interests than those of the Crown. A Genoese by birth, he must have been naturalized, because foreigners were forbidden to serve in such expeditions since August 1500. Nicolas Pérez, who like Vespucci had sailed with Hojeda and La Cosa in 1499–1500, was barred from enlisting with Bastidas because he was "estrangero," possibly Portuguese.[5]

We know that at least three other investors (Juan de Ledesma, García Pérez, Diego Hurtado) took part in the expedition, probably as common sailors, since they received pay for their *marinaje* (seamanship). By doing so, they wished to keep a watchful eye over their investments. This was not an unusual practice by any means; we find more examples of it in other Andalusian voyages.

Both ships carried cannon, and the two *lombarderos* (artillerymen) came from Flanders. They were probably mercenaries who had served in the Spanish army, and were not included in the foreigners forbidden to go to the Indies. The sick and wounded were attended to by a physician and two barbers. The latter not only trimmed hair and shaved beards; they also bled patients and performed minor operations.

According to Bartolomé de la Casas, a young hidalgo from Jerez de los Caballeros (Estremadura) also joined the expedition. He does not appear among the men who were paid after they returned to Seville, in 1503, because he did not go back to Spain but settled in Hispaniola.[6] His name was Vasco Nuñez de Balboa, and he was to become famous later as the discoverer of the Pacific.

Bastidas and Martín de Buniorte were still in Seville on 18 February 1501, when they signed a promissory note for 17,500 maravedis in favor of the merchant Alonso Nuñez.[7] The armada must have sailed shortly after that, very likely before the end of the month, since it reached the vicinity of Santa Marta in May. It probably followed the route traced by Columbus in 1498 (Canaries, Cabo Verde archipelago). On their way to America, the Spaniards sighted an island which they called *Isla Verde* because of the luxuriance of its vegetation. It could have been Barbados or Grenada. The island appears on a map in the 1511 edition of Pietro Martire's *Decades*.

They sailed past the Costa de las Perlas and Coquibacoa without stopping, for they had been strictly forbidden to do so. In addition to La Cosa's expert steersmanship and previous knowledge of the coastline, they must have had favorable winds, for they made excellent time. After reaching the Cabo de la Vela, the western limit of Coquibacoa, they sailed southwest, following the shore, exploring. They discovered Rio Hacha, just south of the Guajira peninsula, where pearls are still fished today. Early in May they reached a land called *Citurma* or *Saturma*, located between the shore and lofty mountains, higher than any peak in Europe, and covered with snow all year round in spite of the tropical climate. Citurma was just east of the present city of Santa Marta, and the mountains that tower over it are the *Sierra Nevada*. In the lowlands and the foothills lived the *Taironas*, one of the most civilized tribes east of the Andes. Their houses and temples were round structures of wood with stone foundations. They had roads paved with slabs, lived on maize and other crops, practiced irrigation, and built aqueducts and reservoirs.[8]

There the Spaniards did some bartering, and the Indians were so friendly that Bastidas left one of his men, Juan de Buenaventura, to live among them, learn their language, and get the lay of the land. No doubt Buenaventura expected to be picked up on the way back, but this did not happen, for man proposes and God disposes. He lived thirteen months among the Indians and became accustomed to their way of life. He finally made his way to Coquibacoa, where he joined Hojeda's second expedition (May 1502). More will be said about him in another chapter.

Leaving Citurma, Bastidas and La Cosa sighted a bay called by the natives *Carimari,* which they baptized *Cartagena.* In the bay they saw the islands of Baru and Codego, and further west a small archipelago which they named *San Bernardo.* Then they sailed south and reached the mouth of the Sinú (or Cenú).

This river flows north between the eastern and middle prongs of the Cordillera Occidental, between the Serrania de las Palomas to the west, and the Serrania de San Jeronimo to the east. The climate is tropical, the annual average temperature being 85° F. Because of torrential rains, parts of the valley are almost constantly flooded; hence the name *cienaga* (lagoon or marsh) which so often appears as a place-name on the maps of that region.

The inhabitants, called *Sinu* or *Zenu,* enjoyed such a warm climate that they could dispense with clothes. The men went naked, except for a penis sheath carved from a mollusk shell or made of gold leaf; the women wore only a skirt that covered them from the waist to the knees. Nevertheless, they were expert weavers, knew about alloys, and were skilled in goldwork. The metal came from Dabeiba, on the Rio Sucio, which is a tributary of the Atrato. Dabeiba is close to the gold mines of the Andes.

The capital or chief center of the Zenu was *Finzenu,* up river, near the modern town of Cienaga Betanci. The great temple of Finzenu could accommodate 1,000 persons and contained 24 tall wooden idols covered with gold leaf and crowned with tiara. In the vast cemeteries that surrounded the town, the tombs contained objects of gold and pottery, for like many primitive nations, the Zenu believed that the deceased should be well provided for before journeying to the Land of the Dead.[9]

Did Bastidas and his men go as far inland as Finzenu? They could have in small boats, but I do not think so. Most probably, they limited themselves to trading with the natives who lived at the mouth of the river or on the Gulf of Morrosquillo, whose flooded shores are lined with a low forest of stilt-rooted mangrove trees. The ambiance was favorable to bartering, since the Zenu were friendly and the Spanish captain well disposed toward them. Andrés Bernáldez relates in his chronicle an almost incredible story. According to him, the Zenu became tired of exchanging their gold for trinkets and asked to have is back. Wishing to avoid violence, Bastidas complied. On the whole, his relations with the Zenu seem to have been friendly. The local cacique invited him to his home and treated him to a chicken dinner.[10]

From the mouth of the Sinu, the Spaniards sailed southwest again. They reached an island which they called *Isla Fuerte;* and it may have been there that Bastidas decided to recoup his previous loss (if we still believe Bernáldez), by kidnapping Indians and holding them for ransom, which was paid out in gold. Very likely the natives did not like it and put up some resistance, hence the name "Strong Island" given to the place by the Spaniards. This hostility may have been the reason why Juan de La Cosa later denounced these Indians as rebels and cannibals. In his indictment he included as well the natives of Barú, Cartagena and San Bernardo, and persuaded the Queen to permit their enslavement (30 October 1503).[11]

Proceeding southward, the Christians reached the Gulf of Urabá. Probably they had been told by the Zenu they would find more gold there, and to be sure, in Urabá, they would be much closer to the source of the metal; by going up the Atrato in canoes or small boats, the gold mines of the Andes could be reached. Bastidas and his men discovered Punta Caribana, which guards the entrance of the gulf on the east side. They also baptized some reefs near the opposite shore *Los Coxos* (the Lame), this being the name often given to groups of small islets or rockets of uneven size or shape.

The Gulf of Urabá is 50 kilometers wide and 70 kilometers long. The east coast is part of the southern continent, while the west side belongs to Central America. Its shores are low and swampy, and luxuriant forests fed by torrential rains reach out to the sea. The climate is hot and unhealthy. In the southwest the Atrato River delta, through its 15 branches, is steadily gaining ground and threatening to close the bottom part of the gulf, turning it into a freshwater lake.

The armada remained a few days in the gulf. The Christians bartered with the Indians and obtained gold. Nine years later, Nuñez de

Balboa was here again, with Diego de Nicuesa and the cartographer Martín Fernández de Enciso. He told the latter: "I remember that in years past, coming down this coast with Bastidas, we entered this gulf, and on the west side to the right, we landed and saw a village (Darien) across a large river, and green and fertile farm land, and its inhabitants did not poison their arrows."[12] Darien was an important Indian settlement, situated just north of the Atrato delta, communicating with it through swamps and channels. On its emplacement Enciso founded the town of *Santa María la Antigua,* which was later abandoned. In 1956 Belgian archaeologists led by King Leopold located the site with the aid of helicopters. They excavated it and found the native village below the ruins of the Spanish town.[13]

After their short stay in Urabá, Bastidas and La Cosa sailed along the coast of Panama. How far west did they go? There is some disagreement among chroniclers and witnesses in the *Pleitos.* Several, including Las Casas, maintain that Bastidas reached a harbor that Columbus was to baptize eighteen months later *Puerto del Retrete.* This site is not far from Puerto Belo, and today is called Puerto de Escrivanos. According to these same sources, the Admiral was there on 26 November 1502, during his fourth voyage, and he found traces that Bastidas had preceded him.[14] Yet another witness in the *Pleitos* quoted La Cosa as saying that he and Bastidas had only reached the *Puerto de Misas* and the *Isla de Piñas* (Pineapple Island),[15] thirty leagues from Darien. The *Puerto de Misas* was in Anachucuna Bay (77° 30'W.), between Cabo Tiburón and Punta Carreto, across the border from Colombia.

Then the Spaniards turned back, because the waters of the Colombia Basin were infested with *teredos,* wood-boring mollusks that played havoc with the hulks of the ships. Bastidas' vessels were greatly in need of repair. For this reason, they abandoned their plan to retrace their steps and pick up Juan de Buenaventura in Citurma, and they headed toward Hispaniola, where they hoped to find relief (July 1501). Before landing there, however, they had to sail to Jamaica, "for with prevailing easterly trades and a westerly set of current there was no use trying to cross the Caribbean to Hispaniola from any point west of Cabo de la Vela."[16]

With difficulty they reached Jamaica where food was obtained. Then the hazardous journey to Santo Domingo was attempted in badly leaking ships. The fleet arrived at a small island one league east of Hispaniola. (It cannot be Navassa, which is too far away; yet, if it is not Navassa, what can it be?). This island was called *Isla del Contramaestre.* There the Spaniards breamed their ships and sailed again; but they ran into contrary winds, and their vessels still took water, so that they were again forced to land near a cape named *Cabo de la Canongia,* where they had to stay one month waiting for better weather. There Bastidas bought food from the natives. He claimed later that he had tried to send a message to Governor Bobadilla, to inform him of his presence in the island, but was unable to contact him. Finally, another attempt was made to sail away, but they ran into one more storm and were driven ashore. The ships were a total loss and had to be abandoned. Bastidas burned his arms and buried his artillery, to keep the Indians from getting hold of them. Then, because of the scarcity of food in the region they had to cross, he divided his men into three platoons, who were going to make their way successively. Thus they would be better able to find food, and they would be less of a burden on the poor Indians.

When they reached Santo Domingo, Bartolomé de las Casas saw them. They brought along two or three chests full of gold, and also some Indians from the Sinu or Urabá, who wandered through the town completely naked, except for their private parts, which they kept in gold sheaths. Bobadilla had Bastidas arrested and ordered an investigation. Just as Columbus had resented Hojeda's presence in Hispaniola two years before, Bobadilla treated Bastidas as an intruder. The latter was accused of landing three times in the island without authorization, of selling swords, spears, daggers, and a grindstone to the natives, and of paying for the food they gave him with clothing and utensils he had brought from Spain, in violation of his capitulation, which forbade him to trade in Hispaniola.

Bastidas denied that he had ever given or sold arms to the natives. He declared that if he had landed three times, it was because he had been forced to do so through bad weather and the sorry state of his ships. He admitted to trading with the natives but only to secure food, guides, and porters; and if he had made small gifts of brass objects or articles of clothing to the caciques, it had been strictly within his prerogatives as captain of their Majesties the King and Queen of Spain. All this he had done to protect his men and to save the valuable cargo he was bringing, which consisted of slaves, gold, brazilwood, clothing, etc., which he estimated to be worth five million maravedis.[17]

Ovando, who had just succeeded Bobadilla as governor of Hispaniola, wisely refrained from passing judgment. Since his predecessor was about to depart for Spain with the fleet that had just brought the new governor, the latter decided that Bastidas, his men, and his gold would also embark on the same ships. The armada left Santo Domingo in July 1502. Columbus, who was there on his way to Central America, predicted a storm and suggested that the departure of the fleet be postponed; but Bobadilla, who had so roughly handled the Genoese two years before and despised him, dismissed his warning with a shrug. The sailing took place on schedule. Bobadilla's flagship, the *Capitana,* carried a light that served as rallying point for the more than 20 vessels that formed the armada. The storm predicted by Columbus materialized. One night the light disappeared, and so did the *Capitana,* which went down with all hands on board including Bobadilla. The other vessels scattered in the wind and went "wherever Our Lord was pleased to guide them." Some reached Cadiz; others found refuge in Lisbon or in Galicia. Still others returned to Santo Domingo.[18]

Bastidas landed at Cadiz in September 1502, bringing with him 150 marcos (75 pounds) of gold, much of it in alloys. Since he came under indictment, he was forced to give security and post bonds to make sure he would not avoid trial. He had nothing to fear since he had not lost the royal favor. He went to the Court to report to the Sovereigns and stand trial. Some time in 1503 (we don't know the exact date), the Royal Council absolved him of all charges against him; and on 29 January 1504, he obtained an *ejecutoria,* a decree enforcing the decision of the Council.[19]

Meanwhile, Bishop Fonseca had received instructions to take over Bastidas's booty, liquidate the assets, pay the crews and the investors. Antonio de Escalante and Martín de Buniorte received a total of 190,500 maravedis for their two ships, which had been lost. The King's share (one fourth of the net) amounted to 87,654 maravedis, which means that the profits without the King's fourth were 262,962 maravedis. Once the flat guarantee of 100,000 maravedis to the investors had been set aside, this left 162,962 maravedis to be split into three parts of 54,380 maravedis each, one for the shipowners, one for the crews, and the last for the investors. On the strength of a total investment amounting to 377,547 maravedis, 54,380 would have represented a 14 per cent dividend; but only 10 per cent was paid.[20] The extra money (17,666 maravedis) may have gone to the captain (Bastidas) and to the chief pilot (La Cosa), who were entitled to a bonus, to be deducted from the investors' percentage, as was the custom in such cases. We must also keep in mind that, over and above the 10 per cent dividend already mentioned, the investors also shared the 100,000 guarantee assigned to them. This sum, divided among them in the same fashion, should have brought each of them an additional 18 per cent, so that the total profit amounted to about 28 per cent of their investments.

As for the 30 quintals of brazilwood that Bastidas had left behind in Hispaniola, it was brought to Spain in Alfonso Martín de la Gorda's caravel the following year (1504). The market was saturated, and the prices were low. Alonso Rodríguez, Bastidas's associate, sent small quantities of it to Flanders and Genoa to see if it would sell better there than in Spain.[21] We don't know if such transactions met with success.

Bastidas and Las Cosa were rewarded by the Crown. Each was promised an annual rent of 50,000 maravedis to be paid out of the revenues derived in the future from Urabá and the Sinu;[22] but before they could collect it, Urabá would have to pay for itself, which might mean a long wait. In addition, La Cosa was appointed *alguazil mayor* (chief constable) of Urabá.[23] There again, his appointment would not become effective until there was organized government in that province, and this might take a long time. Not much outside of gold could be expected to be produced in these lands. As Bernáldez put it: "in all that he (Bastidas) discovered, there is no iron, nor anything that is made of it, no wool, no thread except cotton, no tiles, no bricks, not a single man who can read, for they are all savages without law and without handwriting."[24] Of course, the discovery of gold mines would make up for the lack of everything else and would make the colonization of the country worthwhile.

In the summer of 1503, news reached the Court that Portuguese ships had gone to the land discovered by Bastidas, and had brought back brazilwood and slaves. It was also rumored that the King of Portugal had ordered the building of a fortress in Paria. Juan de la

Cosa and Ochoa de Isasaga were sent secretly to Lisbon to check on such rumors. Unfortunately, we don't know the outcome of their mission, except that La Cosa was jailed for a short time by order of the King of Portugal.[25]

As for Bastidas, he acquired the reputation of being a fair dealer who treated the natives humanely. In an age when cruelty to the Indians was the rule rather than the exception, he stood out from Hojeda, La Cosa, and the brothers Guerra. Las Casas, who was his friend, is largely responsible for picturing him in so favorable a light. Nevertheless, we must keep in mind that Bastidas brought back Indian "slaves" to Spain. Were they meant to learn the language and return to their homeland to serve as guides or interpreters? Possibly.

8   Hojeda, Vergara, and Campos
      1502–1503

We have seen that Hojeda returned from his first voyage in June 1500. At the Court he displayed some *piedras verdes* (emeralds) he had found in Coquibacoa, and he offered to bring more. Not to be outdone by Cristóbal Guerra, he also mentioned pearl fisheries and gold mines. He gave such a glowing description of the land he had discovered that the Catholic Sovereigns assented to a second voyage with as many as ten ships, and wrote the customary letter to Fonseca, asking him to negotiate the terms of a new capitulation with Hojeda (28 July 1500).[1] The latter, however, was short of cash and credit, for his first expedition had not brought him much profit. It took him ten months to secure enough financial backing to be in a position to deal with Fonseca; but during that period the royal favor did not falter. On 10 March 1501, he was granted permission to bring from Hispaniola 30 quintals of brazilwood and sell them in Spain. Twenty of the 30 quintals were an outright gift from the Crown, the other ten being in payment for a stallion Columbus had taken from him.[2]

The capitulation with Fonseca is undated, but it must have been obtained toward the end of May 1501. It was confirmed by Isabel and Fernando on 8 June. Two days later, Hojeda was appointed governor of Coquibacoa with jurisdiction civil and criminal, and the power to name and remove all officials.[3]

The capitulation contains some interesting clauses. First of all, Hojeda was strictly forbidden to land on the Costa de las Perlas. The limits of that land were the *Frailes* in the east, and the *Farallón* in the west (the *Frailes* are a small archipelago east of Margarita; as for the *Farallón,* it is a rocky islet near Cape Codera). It was the coast discovered in 1499 by Peralonso Niño and Cristóbal Guerra. From it they had brought a lot of pearls.

Once he had bypassed the Costa de las Perlas, Hojeda was to sail westward, keeping close to the shore and planting at intervals markers bearing the arms of Fernando and Isabel as a proof that the land belonged to Spain, and as a warning for the English to keep out, for the Spanish ambassador in London had reported that the English had discovered lands in the north and were moving south along the coast.

In Coquibacoa Hojeda was to collect all the emeralds he could find. He was also to locate the pearl fisheries and the gold mines he had been gloating about and put them in operation. All the gold, alloys and precious stones, pearls, spices, and drugs he could obtain, all the strange animals, birds, and fish he could capture, would be taken back to Spain without paying any duty. After deduction of the costs, he could keep four fifths of the proceeds; the other fifth would go to the royal treasury. No slaves were to be brought back except by special permission.

As a reward for his services past, present, and future, Hojeda was to receive an annual rent of half the income derived from the province of Coquibacoa, provided that this half of the revenue did not exceed 300,000 maravedis. Also, in compensation for his efforts to ward off the English, he was granted perpetual ownership of six leagues of land in Managua, south-central province of Hispaniola, to plow and reap as he wished; but the mines and harbors that might be included in this grant would be Crown property.

No limit was set on the number of ships he could fit out. He finally sailed with four.

Hojeda had succeeded in obtaining his license because he had convinced Fonseca he had enough credit to defray the costs of the expedition. For that purpose, he had formed a *compañia* with two wealthy merchants, Juan de Vergara (of Basque extraction but resid-

ing in Seville), and García de Campos (or de Ocampo), a cloth
dealer who also lived in Seville. All three were to be equal partners
in the enterprise. Each was to provide one third of the capital and
make it available before 15 August, for the freighting of the ships,
the hiring of the crews, the purchase of supplies, etc. Each would also
receive one third of all the profits, including the annual rent of half
the revenue of Coquibacoa, which had been granted to Hojeda in the
capitulation. The latter, however, reserved for himself only the six
leagues of land assigned to him in Hispaniola.

All three would share in the management of the expedition. All the
decisions were to be taken jointly. If on some matters there was no
unanimity, a majority of two would prevail; but Hojeda reserved for
himself the title of *capitan general* and the government of Coquibacoa. As such he would be entitled to the second best jewel in addition to his share of the profits, the best being set aside for the Crown.
The agreement would be valid for two years. None of the three associates could withdraw during that period. If one of them did, he would
have to pay 500 gold castellanos and forfeit his investment.[4]

The armada consisted of four ships, whose names are given here
with those of their respective captains:

La Granada	Juan de Vergara
La Antigua	García de Campos
La Magdalena	Pedro de Hojeda
La Santa Ana	Don Hernando de Guevara

Pedro de Hojeda was Alonso's nephew. He disappeared with his ship
when sent on a mission and was never heard of again. Another
relative of Alonso, a brother-in-law named Diego de Dueñas, also
sailed with the armada, but we don't know in what capacity. As for
Alonso, he did not exercise the direct command of any vessel, but he
had his headquarters on *La Antigua,* Campos' caravel.

The four masters were Pedro de Vergara (*Granada*), Lope Ortiz de
Urquizo, Antón Vidal (*Antigua*), and Miguel Vizcaino. There were
at least five pilots: Antón García, Bartolomé Hernández, Francisco
Gómez, Juan López, and Diego Martín. Perhaps more sailed with
the fleet, for there may have been two on each vessel.

Hojeda must have been very confident of finding gold, for he took
along at least five *plateros* (silver or goldsmiths): Hernando del

Rincón, Francisco Gutiérrez, Lorenzo de Ahumada, Francisco de Virnes, and Pero Pardo. Later they turned against him when they failed to find any precious metal in Coquibacoa.

There were also three *escrivanos* (clerks): Juan Luis, García Fernández de Coto, and Diego de Entramasaguas; and three *veedores* (comptrollers): Diego de Conca, Alonso de Arce, and Hernando Rios, who were to watch over the gold, pearls, and precious stones acquired during the voyage and keep them in special trunks or safes. In addition, there was a seventh man who was both *escrivano* and *veedor*. His name was Juan de Guevara, probably a relative of Don Hernando, a member of the aristocratic family Ladrón de Guevara. He was a protégé and appointee of hte Crown, with a yearly salary of 25,000 maravedis.[5] He died during the expedition.

Over and above the usual number of carpenters, caulkers, and coopers, we find a blacksmith, a cobbler, a swordsmith, and an apothecary (Diego de Montedoca). Several physicians were also on board, but I have been unable to identify them. One of them may have been the *bachiller* Pero Sánchez.

The total number of the members of this expedition may have been close to 150. There was no lack of experience among them, for quite a few had served in other armadas. The captain Hernando de Guevara, the pilots Diego Martín and Juan López, the escrivano Juan Luis and a number of sailors had already served with Hojeda on his first voyage. One of the masters, Antón Vidal, had gone with Niño and Cristóbal Guerra to the Costa de las Perlas, and the pilot Antón García had sailed with Vélez de Mendoza and Luis Guerra. Some soldiers also went along, to guard the fort that Hojeda proposed to build.

The fleet must have sailed from Cadiz early in January 1502. After making stopovers in Gran Canaria and Gomera, it reached Santiago Island in the Cabo Verde archipelago. Campos and Vergara landed there with some of their men to look for food. A disturbance occurred between them and the townfolk; one of the caulkers deserted or was seized by the local authorities. Hojeda asked for his return, but the governor refused, alleging that the man was a Portuguese. Shots were fired by both sides, and the Spaniards boarded five Portuguese vessels anchored in the harbor and ransacked them for food and rigging. Later Campos and Vergara made Hojeda responsible for the fray, while he put the blame on them. He claimed he had fired his cannon in self-defense, to protect his ships as they were leaving the harbor.

The expedition reached Paria in March. Hojeda had his ships run aground in some marshes where they were careened. Then he sailed westward toward Coquibacoa, along the Costa de las Perlas, where he had strictly been forbidden to land, except in the case of extreme necessity. No doubt the scarcity of food constituted a case of *force majeure,* for a landing was ordered on the coast of Curiana. Beside food, each man was allowed to bring back a jar, a jug, and a hammock. During his trial, Hojeda maintained that he had forbidden his men to slash the Indians; they could only slap them on the shoulder with the blade of their swords. Nevertheless, six natives were killed. And since the long voyage from home had sharpened the sexual appetite of the Spaniards, they kidnapped some young girls. Campos got one and Vergara two. As for Hojeda, according to testimoney given in his favor, all he obtained from this foray was one hammock.

A few days later Juan de Vergara made another landing; but the Indians offered stiff resistance and killed 16 of his men.[6]

On 12 March, Hojeda estimated that he had reached Cape Codera and the western end of the Costa de las Perlas, and he ordered the comptroller Diego de Conca to make an inquiry. Conca questioned the men who had been there before with Niño and Cristóbal Guerra, and he reported that indeed they had reached the end of the Costa de las Perlas; therefore, Hojeda could land wherever he wished. An official procèsverbal of the proceedings was drawn up by the *escrivano* Diego de Entramasaguas. And since it was 14 March, a landmark to port was baptized *Cabo de San Lorenzo.*[7]

At that time the fleet had been reduced to three vessels, for the *Santa Ana* had been lost from sight in the vicinity of Margarita and had been missing for several days. Her commander Don Hernando explained later that, because of an approaching storm, he had anchored near the shore of the island and had spent the night there. Was he telling the truth, or had he been tempted to indulge in some poaching, that is, in some pearl fishing? On 12 March, as the *Santa Ana* was still missing, Hojeda sent his nephew Pedro, captain of the *Magdalena,* and Juan de Vergara, captain of the *Granada,* to look for the lost vessel.[8] Hojeda was later accused of sending his nephew to Margarita, not to locate Guevara, but to look for pearls, in spite of the interdiction to do so that was included in his capitulation. A few days later Pedro,

Vergara, and Guevara rejoined Hojeda separately. Vergara claimed he had seen Pedro bartering for pearls. The *Santa Ana* sailors had an interesting story to tell. One day when they were anchored three or four leagues from land, between two small reefs where nested a multitude of birds of various kinds, they killed with their oars some 40 of them in less than a quarter of an hour.

After the Puerto de Codera (baptized two years earlier *Aldea Vencida* by Hojeda), the Christians reached *Puerto Flechado,* where Hojeda and Vespucci had had an encounter with Indians in 1499, and which Navarrete identifies with Chichiriviche. They spent the first half of April at a site they called *Valfermoso,* which may have been in the vicinity of Punta Zamuro. It must have been during their stay there that they paid a visit to the *Isla de los Gigantes* (Curaçao), where they took nothing, and saw little gold but a lot of brazilwood. In Valfermoso, they had a clash with the natives, in which one of the *escrivanos* was killed; but a much greater danger than the hostility of the Indians was the scarcity of food. To remedy this, it was decided that Juan de Vergara would sail on the *Granada* to Jamaica to buy bread from the natives. He was expected to be back within one month at the latest, and to rejoin the armada at Maracaibo Lake or at the Cabo de la Vela.[9]

After his departure, the fleet, reduced to three vessels, sailed along the coast toward the Cabo de la Vela, but it did not reach that cape, for on the way it stopped at a spot Hojeda found suitable for the building of a fort, which he called *Santa Cruz* (3 May). Some historians have identified this place with Bahia Honda, a bay on the northeast shore of the Guajira peninsula, near Punta Gallina. At first glance, this identification seems very sound; but Hojeda testified in his trial that he had built his fort on Paraguana peninsula.[10] Moreover, from other documents it can be deduced that on his second voyage he did not reach Guajira and did not go beyond Paraguana. This peninsula is east of the Gulf of Venezuela. It is 35 miles long and 25 wide. It could well be mistaken for an island, for it is connected to the mainland by a narrow isthmus 3 miles wide and 20 miles long. About 22 miles southeast of Cape San Román, there is the bay of Adicora, which may have been the site of Hojeda's Santa Cruz. It was called the *Puerto de Paraguana* in the sixteenth century.

In Paraguana dwelt the Caquetio, who also occupied Aruba, Curacão, and Bonaire. They spoke an Arawakan dialect. During the rainy season, when the land was flooded, they lived in pile dwellings, but during the rest of the year, they slept on the ground or in hammocks. The men wore calabash covers and the women woven material to hide their genitals.[11]

By 20 May Juan de Vergara had not returned from Jamaica. The food stores were almost depleted and the situation was alarming. Hojeda decided to send his nephew Pedro, the pilot Juan López, and the Indian girl called Isabel, with 15 men, in search of the *Granada*. According to the instructions he gave them, their mission was twofold. First they were to sail to Jamaica, to see if they could locate Vergara and bring him back. Failing to do so, they should go to the Gulf of Venezuela, and from there sail westward and remain a week at the Cabo de la Vela, on the Guajira peninsula, not only trying to find Vergara, but also looking for pearls. If they still had found no trace of Vergara, they should keep sailing to the west, to a river and to a land called Citurma, trying to bring back some Indians who would eventually serve as guides. As for Isabel, one of the native girls who had been kidnapped or bartered three years before by Hojeda, she was to be well treated but closely watched, and attempts should be made to attract some of her relatives on board. Everywhere along the coast the Indians should be questioned and the land should be examined for any trace of gold and pearls.[12]

Having received their instructions, Pedro de Hojeda and Juan López sailed away on the *Magdalena*. But they and their ship disappeared and were never heard of again. Did they run into a storm, or did Isabel betray them?

Why was Hojeda so concerned with the river and land of Citurma, which were south of the Cabo de la Vela? He had not been there before, since on his previous voyage he had not gone beyond the Cabo de la Vela. Why did he give orders to have that coastline so thoroughly explored? Perhaps it is because he had just heard about it from Juan de Buenaventura, the man Bastidas had left behind in Citurma, and who had made his way to Santa Cruz after spending 13 months among the Indians. No doubt, he must have told Hojeda about the possibility of finding gold in Citurma and pearls at Rio Hacha. On the other hand, Buenaventura's arrival gave birth to rumors that Hojeda's Santa Cruz was outside Coquibacoa, in the land discovered by Bastidas in 1501; but both Buenaventura and Hojeda denied it.[13]

Meanwhile, the situation in Santa Cruz was worsening. Because of the climate, many men were ill with fever and a number of them died. Hernando de Guevara almost never left his ship and fearing for his health and his life refused to go inland. Hojeda had taken control of the food stores and of the rationing, claiming that the *despenseros* (stewards) were unfair in their distribution; but he in turn was accused of favoring his friends. The walls of the fort were being built of mud, for there was plenty of it because of the rains. To protect the storehouse Hojeda had three bastions erected, and in each he mounted a cannon. Pedro de la Cueva, García de Campos, and Hernando de Guevara were appointed commanders of the three bastions. The men, weakened by fever and lack of food, complained of the hard work, which they considered unnecessary since a palisade would have been sufficient defense against the Indians. But Hojeda did not relent, for his fort was meant to ward off Englishmen and other Europeans. He ruled with an iron hand, helped by an alguazil, a herald, and an executioner, all appointed by him. A soldier accused of murder was sentenced to the loss of his toes. Another had a nail driven through his foot.

The natives of Santa Cruz were hostile, as had been those of Paria, Curiana, and Valfermoso. From their refuge in the swamps, they harassed the Spaniards. One day García de Campos saw some lurking through the trees near his bastion, and he rushed out with his men to drive them off, leaving his position undefended. Hojeda arrived and upbraided Campos for his conduct. He told him "that he should learn how to fight the Indians, that this was not like measuring yards of silk."[14] As a soldier, he had nothing but contempt for Campos the merchant. The latter felt deeply humiliated by these and other remarks. Furthermore, he wanted to protect his investment, and he did not see how it could be done by remaining there, since there was nothing to be gained. Secretly he began plotting against Hojeda.

About 1 June Juan de Vergara returned from Jamaica, bringing with him an abundant supply of cassava bread and other foods. He was greeted as a hero, since his timely arrival averted starvation; but as he toured the encampment, he was greatly dismayed. This was not what he had expected from Hojeda's promises. He too began fearing for his investment, and Campos had no trouble persuading him that something had to be done. For help, they could count on the masters whose ships were rotting in the harbor, and on the *plateros* (goldsmiths) who had found nothing of value in the region. The Basques, who up to now had been neutral but looked on Vergara as their leader, also sided with them. Knowing that they could rely on the majority of the crews, Campos and Vergara decided to take Hojeda by surprise. Two days after his return Vergara invited the *capitán general* aboard his ship, to take stock of the supplies he had brought back. The latter, unsuspecting, came escorted only by an *escrivano*. As soon as he was on board, they seized him. When the two merchants announced his arrest and removal as leader of the expedition, there was general approval. Don Hernando de Guevara at first remained aloof on his vessel, but he finally accepted from Campos and Vergara the post of *veedor* (comptroller), which had become vacant through the death of Juan de Guevara, while retaining command of his ship. This was a disguised bribe, for it meant an additional revenue of 25,000 maravedis a year, which was not to be sneezed at by a proud but poor hidalgo. Hojeda's partisans, led by Pedro de la Cueva and Diego de Entramasaguas, were powerless, since they were outnumbered and had lost control of the ships and foodstores. With the help of the alguazil Pedro Sardo, Hojeda attempted to escape, but he was caught and put in irons. Thus, tough *hombre* though he was, he proved no match for two lowly but wily merchants.

When the order for the evacuation of Santa Cruz was given, Hojeda protested that he wanted to stay and finish the construction of the fort. His faithful aide La Cueva proposed a compromise. Hojeda would be allowed to remain and would be given the smallest of the three caravels and one third of the supplies. At first Campos and Vergara accepted, but soon they changed their minds. They alleged that since they were his bondsmen and had given security for him in Seville, they were responsible for him and he should return with them. Hojeda denied this, claiming that the bonds had been paid with his own money.[15]

The fleet reached the southeast coast of Hispaniola early in September 1502, and Hojeda was handed over for safekeeping to the *comendador* Gallego, founder and chief magistrate of the town of Azua. The ships remained there for several weeks. Rumors were afoot that Campos, wishing to recoup his losses, planned to load the caravels with brazilwood and sell it in Ireland or somewhere else. Meanwhile, according to Hojeda's testimony, Vergara and Campos opened the chests that had been under the guard of the veedors and contained the gold, pearls, and other things of value acquired during the voyage. The whole lot weighed 42 marcs and 20 ounces (about 22 pounds). It was not much, considering that a large part consisted of alloys of slight value. Vergara took out one marc of alloys, which he generously contributed toward the construction of a Franciscan monastery in Santo Domingo. Then he and Campos pocketed the rest.

Toward the end of September, Hojeda—still a prisoner—reached Santo Domingo on the *Granada*. He was freed but made to stand trial. His captivity had lasted four months. The investigation and the ensuing trial dragged through the fall and winter months 1502–1503. When Vergara died, Lorenzo de Ahumada, one of the *plateros,* replaced him as leader of the prosecution. The main witness for the defense was Diego de Entramasaguas, who as a former retainer of Bishop Fonseca, naturally sided with Hojeda. A fair trial was out of the question. Ovando, the governor, like his predecessors Columbus and Bobadilla, considered the newly discovered lands in Central and South America as under his jurisdiction. To him Hojeda was an interloper who should be punished, even though he had a license from the Crown.

Hojeda was accused of cruelty to the Indians and to his own men. He was held responsible for the general hostility of the natives, for the heavy losses in human lives and in supplies, for the gross mismanagement of the expedition, and for landing on the Costa de las Perlas in violation of his capitulation. It was even asserted that his main reason for not wanting to leave Santa Cruz was that he planned to have himself proclaimed King of Coquibacoa. In his defense, he reversed the charges brought against him, accusing Campos and Vergara of cruelty to the Indians, responsibility in the death of many Christians, violation of their agreement with him, insubordination and rebellion.

The *alcalde mayor* (chief justice) of Santo Domingo, Alonso Maldonado, pronounced sentence. He found Hojeda guilty on all counts, and condemned him to the loss of all his gains and investments in the expedition, and to the confiscation of all his personal property. When Hojeda announced he would appeal, he and his chief prose-

cutors and the records of the trial were sent to Spain, where the
King's Council would review the case. Hojeda asked that Juan de
Buenaventura accompany him to testify in the presence of the Catholic
Sovereigns; but the authorities of Santo Domingo refused, on the
ground that since Buenaventura had become accustomed to Indian
food and to the native way of life, his health might be endangered by
restoring him to civilization. Of course, they were afraid that he might
testify in favor of Hojeda.[16]

On 8 November 1503 the Royal Council cleared Hojeda of all
charges and proclaimed him innocent. On 5 February 1504 he secured
a court order for the return of all his goods and moneys that had been
confiscated.[17]

9/10   Cristóbal and Luis Guerra, 1504
Juan de la Cosa and Juan de Ledesma, 1504–1506

The Queen's displeasure with Cristóbal Guerra does not seem to have
lasted very long. He soon was able to clear himself, probably because
Isabel's attitude toward the enslavement of the natives was becoming
more flexible, since in 1503 she admitted the principle that cannibals
and rebellious Indians could be sold into slavery. As early as 1494,
Columbus had suggested that the Caribs would make good slaves,
being allegedly of a sturdier stock than the natives of La Española; but
the Queen had not shared this view, and when the Admiral sent Indians to Spain to be sold, Isabel had set them free. In 1503, however,
she issued a royal *cédula* permitting the enslavement of the Indians
of Cartagena and Urabá.[1] This was the territory that had been discovered two years before by Bastidas and La Cosa. Bastidas was gentle
with the natives and had no trouble with them; but La Cosa was a
man of entirely different mettle, just as harsh as the Guerras. In 1503
he was eager to go back to America and make good the title of chief
constable of Urabá, which had just been granted to him. It was probably his urging that prompted the Queen to change her mind on
Indian slavery in the region, for she had a high regard for him.

Juan de la Cosa was not the only one who wanted to return to the new continent, for Bastidas and Cristóbal Guerra were also applying for capitulations. The Queen was hoping that all three would go together in a single armada, each of them keeping control of his own ships, but under the supervision of a *capitán general* appointed by her, whose duty would be to maintain harmony between the leaders, enforce the terms of their capitulations, and, most important of all, collect from them directly, on the spot, the *cuarto* of their winnings before any deductions of the costs, thus avoiding much of the defrauding that took place in Spain.[2] Cristóbal was willing to associate with La Cosa. Between them, he thought, they could muster ten or twelve vessels. Cristóbal would first go to the Costa de las Perlas, then join with La Cosa in Urabá. From there they would send some ships back home with their booty, and with the other vessels they would proceed further down the coast exploring. Isabel was pleased with this plan, and on 12 July 1503 a tentative agreement was made with Cristóbal. At the same time, the Queen urged the officials of the newly founded Casa de la Contratación to negotiate with La Cosa and others willing to take part in this project.[3]

Nevertheless, the plan fell through, because Juan de la Cosa refused to associate with Cristóbal. He was prepared to sail with three vessels, but only as his own master. He also objected to handing over a quarter of his earnings before deduction of the costs, preferring the old system of paying one fifth of the gross, so he held out for better terms.

Meanwhile, Cristóbal was running into difficulties. Because of the war with France, he had trouble procuring the seven vessels granted him in his tentative capitulation, and he now asked that he be allowed to outfit only four. He had already spent large sums buying wine and hardtack, but he had not been able to outfit his ships because he had accepted to pay one fourth; therefore, capitalists and mariners waited to see if La Cosa would succeed in obtaining a better deal. He also complained that in part payment of 200,000 maravedis owed him by the Crown for his past two voyages he had been forced to accept a stock of faded and moth-eaten secondhand cloth, while the remainder was being paid out to him in brazilwood at a very unfavorable rate, so that he stood to lose trying to sell it, since the price had dropped on the Seville market. But his main source of discontent was the high favor that La Cosa enjoyed with the Queen and Fonseca. All this we know from two letters Cristóbal wrote on 28 September 1503, one to

Don Alvaro de Portugal, chairman of the Royal Council,[4] the other to Bartolomé Ruyz de Castañeda, the Queen's secretary in charge of all the correspondence relating to the Indies.[5] Perhaps as he wrote these letters, he knew that the Queen had already taken the decision to allow La Cosa to sail alone with his three ships, provided he agreed to pay one fourth as Cristóbal had done. Her letter to the officials of the Casa de la Contratación shows her esteem for La Cosa: "Since it is his wish not to go with Cristóbal Guerra, and in view of his merits, I agree to let him go as his own captain with the three ships he says he can fit out, or more if he so wishes, to the Gulf of Urabá and the Costa de las Perlas, provided he gives us as much as Cristóbal Guerra promised, without discounting anything for costs and for the vessels . . ."[6] The Queen was trying to drive a hard bargain; but despite her hope of getting a *quarto,* finally she had to settle for a *quinto.*

On 14 February 1504, La Cosa, Bastidas, and Cristóbal Guerra were granted identical capitulations. The Crown played no favorites. The plan to have them sail jointly had been abandoned. There was little restriction in the lands they could explore; Urabá and the Costa de las Perlas were thrown open to all, only the lands discovered by Columbus or belonging to the King of Portugal remaining taboo. The leaders were to hand over to the Casa de la Contratación one fifth of their gains, without deducting anything for the vessels, the crews, and other costs. The ships were to sail within four months, but it was fairly easy to obtain a postponement.

On their way to America, they were allowed to stop over in Hispaniola to pick up six Indians Bastidas had left there in 1502, to use them as *lenguas* (interpreters), as well as Juan Buenaventura, whom we have already mentioned in the two preceding chapters. In their capitulation, there was also the prohibition to bring back Indian slaves, unless they were from the San Bernardo Islands, Isla Fuerte, Cartagena, and Barú, for the natives of these islands and lands had been officially pronounced cannibals and rebels by the Queen, and therefore, they could be enslaved.[7]

Bastidas did not make use of his capitulation. Instead, on 28 June 1504 he formed a *compañía* with the cloth merchant Alfonso Rodríguez, who had invested money three years before in the Bastidas– Las Cosa expedition. The aim of the company was trade with Hispaniola, Bastidas handling the Santo Domingo end of the business, while Rodríguez remained in Seville. Soon afterward, the former left for Santo Domingo with a cargo that included some mares. Bastidas had invested 95,910 maravedis, and Rodríguez 55,739 in buying the merchandise; one third of the profits was to go to Rodríguez, while Bastidas would keep the other two thirds. In 1505 another cargo of cloth, wine, mares, burros, etc. was shipped by Rodríguez to Bastidas. In 1507 the draper and his wife died of the plague, leaving five young children. After that Bastidas completely forgot about his partnership with Rodríguez, and kept not only the 55,739 maravedis his associate had invested, but also the third of the profits the draper was supposed to receive. Only after years of arduous litigation and a lengthy trial were the heirs of Bastidas sentenced to pay to the heirs of his former partner the 55,739 maravedis of the investment, plus 300 ducados representing one third of the profits (5 January 1534). Bastidas was not the only one guilty of such "oversights," and so many companies complained of the dishonesty of their American agents that edicts were passed in 1514 and 1538 against such malpractices.[8]

Unfortunately for him, Cristóbal Guerra did make use of his capitulation, and he sailed with three ships between 17 May and 18 July 1504. In Sanlúcar de Barrameda, his fleet was inspected by the *comendador* Luis Pinelo, factor of the Casa de la Contratación, who checked the muster roll and the list of supplies.[9] Cristóbal's brother Luis and another resident of Triana called Monroy, who must have been Alonso de Monroy, the Guerras' nephew, went with Cristóbal as his co-captains.

We have very little information concerning this voyage; our main source is Oviedo.[10] It seems that the Guerras sailed along the Costa de las Perlas, bartering with the natives; then they headed toward Urabá, hoping to take advantage of the royal decree that made the Indians of that region fair prey to slave hunters. Las Casas narrates how Cristóbal kidnapped a cacique of the Cartagena area after enticing him on his caravel, and refused to release him unless the cacique's servants filled a hamper with gold valued at 30,000 pesos. The Dominican dwells at length on the cacique's frightful plight while he was a prisoner in the vessel, for he and his servants feared that Cristóbal's rapacity would never be appeased.[11] In the vicinity of Cartagena, Cristóbal made forays inland in search of gold and slaves, but he met with stiff resistance, for the natives of that region were *flecheros* (skilled archers). One day they ambushed him and killed him.

Meanwhile, Juan de la Cosa was making ready to leave. His departure was hampered by legal actions brought against him. He had to answer a summons issued by a discontented backer, who claimed a greater investment than he was given credit for. To avoid further delay the Crown ordered the Count of Cifuentes, *asistente* (chief administrator) of Seville, to press the judges for a quick settlement of all lawsuits involving armadas going to America.[12]

On 11 September 1504 a general meeting of the *compañía* was held. From the minutes we learn that the armada consisted of four ships whose respective masters were Martín de Celaya, Juan Martín de la Cuerda, Tomé Sánchez, and our old friend Cristóbal Tiscareño. It was to sail to the Costa de las Perlas and the Gulf of Urabá. As *capitán general*, La Cosa was to receive a bonus of 2½ per cent of the investment. Since the bonus was estimated at 30,000 maravedis, the capital invested must have been 1,200,000 maravedis. At the end of the document appear the signatures of the investors, including some marks made by persons who could not write. Unfortunately, we don't know how much money each of them put up. Thirty-three of the signatures can be deciphered. Among them we find those of Juan de Ledesma and Juan de Quecedo (or Quicedo), who sailed with the expedition as ship captains; García Pérez de Cabrera, Martín de Torres, Diego Ximenes, Luis de Negrón, and Alfonso Rodríguez, who like Ledesma had previously laid out money in the Bastidas–La Cosa voyage of 1501–1502. We also find the name of Sancho Ortiz de Matienzo, treasurer of the Casa de la Contratación, who signed for his wife María de Villasante and for his nephew Juan de Santiago. In addition, Matienzo signed for "the Holy Church of Seville," to which an investor now deceased had willed his fortune. An individual called Pedro de Moguer also signed for his wife. A third woman appears among the investors: Catalina Centurión, a member of the prosperous Genoese colony of Seville. She attended the meeting and signed her own name.[13]

On 16 September Juan de Quecedo made out his will, dividing his property equally between his wife and his brother.[14] On 18 September Cristóbal Tiscareño was still in Seville, signing a promissory

note for 8,500 maravedis in favor of the *jurado* (justice of the peace)
Diego de Alcocer. Meanwhile, Tiscareño's ship had already reached
Sanlúcar de Barrameda, at the mouth of the Guadalquivir, and was
waiting for him there. The fleet must have sailed shortly after that
date.[15]

The first stopover was in Gran Canaria, where they obtained fresh
meat, water and firewood. After crossing the ocean, they struck land
in Margarita. There they bartered with the natives, who gave them
food and parrots. On the coast of Cumaná they collected very few
pearls; but on the islands to the north (the Curaçao archipelago),
they found much brazilwood and loaded more than 800 quintals on
their ships. Then they went to the Bay of Cartagena, where they
met the armada of the brothers Guerra. Cristóbal was already dead,
killed by the Indians, and Luis was now in charge. He and his men
were suffering from scurvy, "their mouths very sore and damaged by
the bad food they were eating." La Cosa gave them some fresh supplies. Luis was demoralized and wanted to go home, and it was
decided his ships would take back to Spain the brazilwood and slaves
La Cosa had already acquired; but before the expeditions parted,
they made a joint attack on *Codego* Island (today Tierra Bomba) in
the Bay of Cartagena. There they captured 600 Indians, releasing
some who were too old, too young, or too feeble.

Oviedo, who is our main source of information for La Cosa's
voyage, could not help passing judgment on the conduct of the Spaniards: "It seems to me that this manner of exploring and bartering
should be better called laying waste. I do not know if these merchants
were authorized to enslave the people of that land, because they are
idolaters, savages, sodomites, or because they eat human flesh; but I
know that Juan de la Cosa paid for his assault and brigandage in that
same land."[16] This was an allusion to La Cosa's horrible death five
years later on that coast, his body riddled by poisoned arrows.

Leaving Luis Guerra and his ships in Cartagena Bay, La Cosa
sailed southwest to Isla Fuerte, which he plundered. Then he reached
the mouth of the Sinú, kept following the coast, and entered the Gulf
of Urabá, which he and Bastidas had discovered three years before.
The Christians made several forays inland, looking for gold. The
natives usually fled at their approach, abandoned their villages, and
took refuge in the woods. One night, near a lagoon (Aguila Lake?),

the Spaniards found hidden in the woods a large hut, which the Indians used as a meeting place; in it was a chest containing kettle drums and masks that weighed 72 marcs of gold.

So far we have followed Oviedo's matter-of-fact account; but the acquisition by the Spaniards of the kettle drums, the masks, and the other gold objects is described in a much more dramatic and colorful vein by Girolamo Vianello, a pompous and gullible Venetian agent at the Court of Spain. In a report addressed to his government on 23 December 1506, he first writes how La Cosa's expedition reached a strange island divided in the middle by a mountain range. In the northern half lived the Indians while the southern part swarmed with snakes, dragons, and sea serpents. The inhabitants of each half made no attempts to cross over and mix with the others. La Cosa picked up seven natives (in the northern half, of course) to act as guides. The expedition sailed 400 leagues further west, to a land called *Alsechii,* and disembarked there near a village; but instead of running away, the Indians rushed toward the Spaniards to greet them. They told the newcomers that, through a revelation, they had learned how some ships would come from the East, sent by a great King and that, by becoming his subjects, they would acquire immortality. Then the cacique appeared, dressed in a gold breastplate and with gold bells attached to his legs, escorted by twenty Indians wearing gold masks and carrying gold kettle drums; and the cacique said to his escort: "Here are the ships I told you about ten years ago." But at the sight of the seven Indian guides from the island of the serpents the natives became angered and attacked the Spaniards. A clash resulted between the 140 Christians and 5,000 aborigines. When it was over, 700 of the latter were dead, while one Spaniard had been killed by poisoned arrows. The kettle drums, the masks, the bells, and the cacique's armor, weighing in all 800 gold marks, fell into the hands of the invaders.[17]

This episode makes a good story, but how much of it is true? Vianello's account of this voyage is full of errors. For example, he mentions Amerigo Vespucci as one of the leaders of the expedition, but there is positive proof that the Florentine did not leave Spain between 1504 and 1506. Vianello's island of snakes and dragons is probably a misinterpretation of Trinidad, which is separated from the mainland by two narrow straits called Dragon's Mouth and Serpent's

Mouth, names given to them by Columbus during his third voyage. As for the 800 gold marks taken by the Spaniards according to the Venetian, this is a grossly exaggerated evaluation. Oviedo's figure of 72 marks is much nearer the truth.

Vianello's account shows an almost complete lack of knowledge of the Indies. For a diplomat who enjoyed the implicit confidence of Cardinal Cisneros, regent of Castile, the Venetian seems to have been greatly misinformed, although not much more than some diplomats I have known. My feeling is that Vianello's informants were pulling his leg.

From a cacique and other Indian captives, the Christians learned that there was much precious metal on the other side of the gulf, in the province called Darien. They crossed the gulf, and one night they entered a river with their boats, having left their ships off shore. The river in question may have been the Atrato. In a village they seized various gold objects weighing 40 marcs.

It was there, at the mouth of that river, that La Cosa received an appeal for help from the Guerra expedition. Just after leaving Cartagena on its way back to Spain, with its cargo of brazilwood and slaves, Luis Guerra's caravel had run into some reefs and had sunk with most hands on board. The remaining ship commanded by Monroy tried to rejoin La Cosa, but could not make it. Its hulk was worm-eaten, and it leaked so badly that at the entrance of the Gulf of Urabá, on the east side, its crew ran it aground. Monroy dispatched the bergantin with a few men in search of La Cosa.

The latter hurried to the rescue. He reached the spot where Monroy and his crew were beached and picked them up; but his own vessels were in such a sorry state that their pumps could no longer keep them afloat. They too had become the victims of the dreaded *teredo,* the scourge of the tropical seas. La Cosa decided to run them aground near the village of Urabá, not far from the lagoon.

Thus both Guerra brothers died on the coast of Cartagena, in the fall or winter months of 1504–1505, Cristóbal at the hands of the Indians and Luis in the wreck of his ship. In the fate of the two brothers, Las Casas saw the hand of Divine Providence, a punishment meted out to them for their cruel treatment of the natives. As for their nephew Alonso de Monroy, since he was never heard of again, we may take it for granted that he met his Maker in Urabá, a victim of fever or starvation.[18]

The 200 men that remained of both expeditions were stranded on the Urabá beach for almost a year. They had removed from the rotting hulks the artillery, supplies, and anything that could be of use, and with the sails and rigging they made tents. But food was scarce and the natives were hostile. Besides, unused to the climate, more than half of the Spaniards died of disease. The survivors decided to flee this accursed land. They buried the artillery, anchors, and anything they could not carry, and loaded the rest including their gold in the two bergantins and the one boat that could stay afloat. After two days of navigation to the northeast, they reached the harbor of Zamba, north of Cartagena, at a latitude of 10° 54′ N. The Indians fled at their approach and abandoned the village; but since no food could be found, three Spaniards killed a native, planning to eat his flesh. When La Cosa learned of this act of cannibalism, he rushed to the scene, upset the kettle where the human debris were boiling, and upbraided the three Christians for their crime.

After a few days, the Spaniards left Zamba, but they ran into a storm and had to return. They waited for better weather, then decided to attempt the long and hazardous crossing to Hispaniola. After a few days of navigation, the boat became separated from the bergantins and was lost sight of. It eventually made its way to Cuba. The east winds were driving the bergantins toward Jamaica, as La Cosa had experienced four years before, and as also happened to Columbus in 1503. They finally reached Pedro Cays, a group of four islets 40 to 50 miles from the south shore of Jamaica, at a longitude of about 77° W. Many pelicans were nesting among the rocks. They were very tame. The sailors seized some with their hands, killed them, and ate them. They also caught a quantity of fish and spent the night there. Today many birds still nest on Pedro Cays. This accounts for their abundant guano deposits that are leased for mining by the Jamaican authorities.

The Spaniards left again at dawn and soon saw a mountain. It must have been Great Pedro Bluff, which is 540 feet high and serves as a landmark; behind it rise the Santa Cruz mountains, whose highest peak, Malvern, reaches a height of 2,378 feet. They sailed toward it and anchored in a bay nearby, not knowing where they were. The bay may have been Great Pedro Bay, or Starve Gut Bay, or Black River Bay, all exposed to southwesterly winds, which sometimes cause a heavy swell that sweeps the shore.[19] The Spaniards disembarked there, and fed on the mollusks they found on the beach.

By the time they reached Jamaica, their number had dwindled to fifty. Leaving twenty mostly sick men on the beach to guard the vessels and the gold, La Cosa and Ledesma took the other thirty inland. Each man carried his buckler and sword, and for fire power, the whole group relied on one musket and two crossbows. They advanced about three leagues and reached a village of ten or twelve huts. Most of the Indians fled, but some remained and through sign language, the Christians asked for food. They were given cassava bread, wild cherries, and *hutias*.[20] Two Indians were dispatched to the beach with food for the men who had remained there. Then the Spaniards moved to another village only one and one half leagues away. The natives did not flee, but hid their women and children. There the Christians obtained more cassava bread and fish, but before departing they received bad news. During their absence, a wester had hit the beach and a heavy swell had run both bergantins aground. The smaller ship was not badly damaged, but the larger one had been torn apart.

Leaving their men to search for more food inland, La Cosa and Ledesma rushed back to the beach. They loaded their provisions on the bergantin that was still serviceable, and put on board the sick with a small crew sufficient to man the vessel. They knew now that they were on Jamaica, and that Hispaniola stood to the east of them. La Cosa appointed Juan de Quecedo and Andrés Morales captain and pilot of the bergantin, and gave them orders to sail along the southern shore of the island until they reached its easternmost point. Then they were to cross over to Hispaniola, leave the sick there, and return to Jamaica to pick up the gold and the rest of the men. The bergantin sailed away; but when it reached Morant Point, Quecedo and Morales disagreed, and instead of carrying out their instructions, they decided to wait for La Cosa's arrival.

The latter, with other Spaniards and some thirty Indian porters, started on foot toward Morant Point. The porters carried the gold, the food, and the goods for barter; their loads were still almost intact, since the gold had been ill gained, obtained by force or threat, rather than through barter. Since the Spaniards were so few, the natives were tempted to do away with them, and several traps were laid, which the invaders carefully avoided. Once, in the country of Cacique Cabonito, the Indians planned to kill the Christians in their sleep; but the latter, suspecting treachery, refused to spend the night in the village and went on. Their escort had grown considerably, because natives from all parts of the island had come to take part in the plot and enjoy the fun; but although they appeared most friendly and most eager to serve, the Spaniards were not fooled. One day, as the caravan had reached the mouth of a river, the Christians were invited to lay down their arms, bathe, and relax, but La Cosa and Ledesma ordered eight of their men to seize the four caciques who commanded the porters, and to chain them together. This coup de force terrified the Indians who fled in all directions; but later that day, they killed three Christian stragglers, precisely the three who had practiced cannibalism in Zamba, a well-deserved punishment according to Oviedo. The following night all the porters deserted, but the Spaniards replaced them with ten natives they had captured in a village. To terrify the Indians, they set fire to one of the houses; the fire spread quickly, and the whole village went up in smoke.

La Cosa and his men finally reached the district of Cacique Mayaco. There they learned that the bergantin was waiting for them nearby at Morant Point. They loaded their gold and embarked in the bergantin, and a few days later they reached Santo Domingo. Between forty and forty-five of them were still alive; but their number was swelled by the arrival of the fifteen who had reached Cuba in the boat. With their gold freighting a ship to return home offered no problem. We know that they were back in Seville before 13 March 1506.[21]

During the eighteen months their voyage lasted, the survivors had endured incredible hardships. They had seen their companions drown, die of starvation, disease, exhaustion, or at the hands of natives. They had lost their ships, their slaves, their brazilwood; but they had saved their gold, their precious gold. "You who can read, see how few of the many Christians were left, and how they managed to survive; and realize how much costs this gold, and how it is obtained in those parts and how the survivors enjoyed it quietly, without giving any share of it to the families of the dead and drowned, to enrich three or four individuals, and particularly Juan de la Cosa who kept the greater part of it, for which he was to pay later with his life."[22]

These are the words of Gonzalo Fernández de Oviedo, who obtained his very detailed account of the voyage from his friend Juan de Ledesma, one of the chief participants and investors. Back in his native city of Seville, enjoying a glass of wine or two in his home, in his store, or in the water-front taverns, the merchant turned explorer must have had many hair-raising stories to tell his relatives, friends, and business associates, about his harrowing but profitable experience.

We have proof that the expedition more than paid for itself and the survivors struck it rich: one month after his return, on 7 April 1506, Juan de Quecedo loaned 150 ducados "of fine gold, weighed exactly at the rate of 375 maravedis per ducado," to Francisco de Castillo, master of the *Santa Maria de Guia*, who was planning to take a cargo of merchandise to Puerto de la Plata, in Hispaniola.[23]

We know exactly how much gold La Cosa declared (he probably brought more) to the officials of the Casa de la Contratación when he returned to Spain. It weighed 122 marcs (61 pounds), and was valued at 2,459,611 maravedis. It included all kinds of gold objects: drums, masks, vases, jingle bells, earrings, greaves, hatchets, and leaves. The King's share (one fifth of the gross) amounted to 491,922 maravedis. Not all of the King's quinto was melted however, because Fernando's curiosity had been aroused, and he asked Sancho de Matienzo, treasurer of the Casa de la Contratación, to send him a kettle drum, a mask, and a hatchet.[24] Out of the royal share, 50,000 maravedis were paid out to La Cosa, and a similar amount to Bastidas, in virtue of an order issued three years earlier, granting each of them a sum annually for life, from the revenues of Sinú and Urabá; but it is doubtful that this sum was ever paid to them again.[25]

11   Alonso de Hojeda and Pedro de la Cueva
1505–1506

In spite of the disastrous outcome of his second voyage, Alonso de Hojeda had not lost the royal favor. Isabel and Fernando remembered how faithfully he had served them in the past, and how his father before him had been a staunch supporter in the war against Portugal and the partisans of "La Beltraneja." The blame for the failure of the 1502 enterprise was put on Campos and Vergara. Besides, Hojeda was anxious to redeem himself. On 30 September 1504 he was granted another capitulation.[1]

In that document, Hojeda was allowed to go to the Costa de las Perlas, Coquibacoa, Urabá, or anywhere else, excepting the lands belonging to the King of Portugal and those discovered by Columbus. On the site of his 1502 fort, or on any other location that might prove appropriate, Hojeda would erect a fortress strong enough to be defended by a few men. It was to be built and maintained by him for three years at his expense; after that time, the Crown would take it over. The garrison would consist of 50 men, whose pay would be provided by the royal treasury for the first five months. Afterward, for the next 31 months, the soldiers would be paid out of the local revenues. In exchange, Hojeda would be governor of the province and captain of the fortress; he would receive an annual salary, and he would be granted an extensive stretch of land in Hispaniola.

The text of the license makes it clear that the first and foremost aim of Hojeda's mission was not discovery but occupation and defense. There had been a hint of this in his previous capitulation (1501), when he had been ordered to ward off the English; and if in that voyage he had undertaken to build a fort, although no mention of it was made in his capitulation, it must have been suggested to him in private conversations with the Sovereigns or with Fonseca. Now there was no doubt that Hojeda's third voyage would be essentially political and military, but to succeed, the new province would have to be made productive. It would have to pay for itself since most of the funds would have to come from the local treasury, a very unlikely prospect.

On Hojeda's shoulders fell the burden of financing the expedition. He had to find backers, a hard task in view of his previous failure. To make it easier for him, it was agreed that seven investors of Hojeda's own choosing would, like him, receive extensive grants of land in Hispaniola. One of the chosen was Pedro de la Cueva, Hojeda's *paisano* (compatriot), since both were from Cuenca. La Cueva had already taken part in the 1502–1503 voyage, and throughout he had stood by his chief. Hojeda promoted him to be second-in-command of the new expedition.

The capitulation also included the usual provision for the Crown's share of the profits, with varying figures: one sixth of the gross in lands discovered by Hojeda, one fifth in those discovered by others. These terms favored Hojeda, if we compare them to those granted to leaders of other expeditions. His armada was to consist of two or three ships and was to sail within six months.

Attempts were also made to recuperate the gold, alloys, pearls, and merchandise that Hojeda had gained in his previous voyage, and which had been confiscated by Ovando and handed over to Campos, Ahumada, and the heirs of Juan de Vergara, since Hojeda had been sentenced in Santo Domingo to the loss of all his gains and personal property. Later he had been cleared of all charges by the Royal Council, and had obtained, on 3 February 1504, an *ejecutoria,* a decree enforcing the Council's decision in his favor. But justice is slow when it has to cross the seas; moreover, Ovando, who did not like Hojeda, played deaf and allowed Hojeda's enemies to keep their ill-gotten gains. The King had to write several times to the governor of Hispaniola, instructing him to send to Seville the confiscated goods and moneys, which were to be used to liquidate Hojeda's debts, for he still owed considerable sums to the crew members who had accompanied him on his ill-fated expedition (21 and 28 September, 5 October 1504; 10 September 1505).[2]

Hojeda also received from the Crown 200,000 maravedis to pay the 50 soldiers who were to sail with him. Each was to collect 26 maravedis and 4 *cornados* a day (15 November 1504).[3] Hojeda had to give security that he would use the sum as ordered, and one of his bondsmen was Charles de Valera, son of Mosen Diego, the chronicler. Like Hojeda, the Valeras were from Cuenca. In addition, Hojeda was authorized to take with him six white slaves "born in our Kingdom of Castile."[4] White slaves were common in Spain as a result of the conquest of Granada, for the population of whole cities like Malaga had been enslaved. At the time of his death (1509), Gonzalo Gómez de Cervantes, corregidor of Jerez and uncle of Bishop Fonseca, owned ten white slaves and three black ones.[5]

Needless to say, Hojeda was also duly appointed "governor of the said land and coast of Coquibacoa and Urabá from the Cape of the Isleo to the Coxos, which is the Cape of the Gulf of Urabá to the west inclusive." This left the Costa de las Perlas out of his jurisdiction, perhaps because it was felt that Cristóbal Guerra had a special claim on it, or because the Crown wanted to keep it as a sort of royal preserve, as was the case later with Cubagua, where the pearl fisheries belonged to the King and were a state monopoly.

Hojeda was to sail before 31 March 1505. When it became clear that he could not make it, he applied for a two-month delay, which was granted on 10 March.[6] On the same day, the King confirmed his capitulation. Yet this prolongation was not enough, for the fleet did not leave until after 6 June. On that day were purchased three locks "which are to be put on the three chests which are to go in the three caravels which are to sail with Hojeda on his voyage of discovery."[7] The keys were to be kept by the three *veedores* appointed by the Casa de la Contratación. On 16 September the King complained that he had not been informed of Hojeda's departure. Therefore, the armada must have sailed before that date.[8]

Of the voyage itself, almost nothing is known. Hojeda did some bartering and pearl fishing, but the results were meager. We learn this through two entries in the registers of the Casa de la Contratación. On 11 May 1506, the treasurer Sancho de Matienzo received 3 marcs, one ounce and 5 eighths of pearls, in a sealed pouch that Alonso de Sepulveda had brought in his ship, keeping it carefully locked in his safe. It was part of the King's *quinto,* which Hojeda had sent to Hispaniola from "la costa del mar oceano." On 15 July Carlos de Hontiveros handed over to Matienzo 2 marcs, 4 ounces and 7 eighths, which he had brought from Hispaniola. It was another part of the King's share of the pearls, which Hojeda and his associates had fished or bartered in Urabá and Coquibacoa. Most of it consisted of beads and *aljofar* (irregularly shaped pearls) of little value.[9]

Politically, the results of Hojeda's third voyage were even more disappointing. His partners quickly dissuaded him from repeating his previous mistake, from settling in a land that seemed devoid of economic prospects, incapable of providing the short-range benefits they had been hoping for. If he had entertained the idea of rebuilding his fort in Santa Cruz or elsewhere, he soon gave it up. As for the 50 soldiers who accompanied him, we have no information of what happened to them; but we can safely guess that he took them with him to Hispaniola, where he, La Cueva, and his other backers decided to claim the lands which had been assigned to them by royal decree. They settled on their *encomiendas* (grants), and began to live like gentlemen farmers, amidst dwindling Indian villages and fields of corn and cassava, raising cattle and half-breed children in their spare time, for their main business was looking for gold. Not for long, however, for Hojeda. In 1508 he was reappointed governor of Urabá, and went on another disastrous expedition in which his second-in-command La Cosa was killed and he was grievously wounded by poisoned arrows. Then, grown wiser through this sad experience, he returned to his *encomienda,* giving up all political ambitions, nursing his wounds, and commending his soul to God, until he passed away dressed in the robe of a Franciscan monk (end of 1515).

Hojeda's third expedition marks the end of the Andalusian voyages. The primary aim of such undertakings was no longer an incentive, since the whole north shore of South America had turned out to be one continuous coastline, without a strait or passage to India. Moreover, peaceful trading with the Indians was no longer possible. The time was past when Cristóbal Guerra and Peralonso Niño could amass quietly a fortune in pearls, through the bartering of worthless trinkets. The natives, so trusting at first, had learned that the coming of the European invaders meant exploitation or extermination. Although their wooden swords and bamboo spears were no match for steel weapons, they were ready to resist, and they would have to be subdued by force. This meant the use of troops, which only the government could provide. After conquest and pacification were achieved, the merchants could come in again.

The first attempt to take possession and colonize was made in 1508, when two provinces were carved out of the new continent: Veragua and Urabá; and soldiers, settlers, and government officials moved in. The first results were disastrous, because the Indians poisoned their arrows, but in the long run they had to submit. All this required massive man power and huge sums of money that private enterprise could not provide.

To be sure, discovery and exploration still flourished, but in other zones. In 1505, an expedition under the leadership of Yañez Pinzón and Amerigo Vespucci was projected. Its goal was the *Espicieria* (land of Spices) but it was canceled the following year. In 1509 Yañez Pinzón and Diaz de Solis tried to find a westward passage through Honduras and Guatemala. They failed, but discovered part of Yucatan. Solis went on another search in 1514 through the Rio de la Plata, and died in the attempt. Finally, Magellan succeeded in 1519. Although private participation was sought, and bankers and merchants invested large sums in these undertakings, the greater part of the cost had to be covered by the royal treasury; and because of the political implications of such voyages, only government officials could organize and lead them. We have seen that at least eleven Andalusian voyages took place. Eleven is the minimum figure; is it also the maximum? Or can we assume that there may have been more? Some ships freighted by the Crown may have been sent on special missions to various parts of the newly discovered continent. For example, a government vessel may have visited the coast between the Orinoco and the Amazon. This territory had been assigned to Yañez Pinzón as part of his governorship on 5 September 1501; but in the capitulation, the rulers of Spain had reserved the right to send some of their own ships to that coast, provided they paid Yañez one fifth of the profits. They may have taken advantage of that clause, for the pilot Andrés de Morales testified in the *Pleitos* that he had explored the coast from the Amazon to Paria; and from his own testimony we know that he had not been there with Yañez or with Lepe. His voyage to the Amazon, or some other in the same region may explain the presence on that section of the La Cosa map of a large number of place-names that bear no relation to the previous explorations of Vespucci, Yañez Pinzón, and Diego de Lepe.[10]

In the testimony he gave in the *Pleitos de Colón* in 1513, Francisco de Porras testified that he had gone by order of the Crown to the pearl fisheries of Cumaná, but this could have been Cristóbal Guerra's voyage of 1500–1501.[11] Porras possibly went along as *veedor* as he did two years later in Columbus' fourth and last voyage.

As to private clandestine expeditions to the north shore of South America, we do not possess a single record. Some must have sailed, however, or must have attempted to do so, for an edict from the Crown (3 September 1501), which strictly forbade such undertakings, was proclaimed through the streets of Seville, Las Palmas, and Santo Domingo.[12] After the return to Spain of the Niño–Guerra caravel, there was much enthusiasm for discovery. Columbus was in Spain in 1501 when capitulations were granted to Hojeda, Yañez, Lepe, and Escalante, and he, who had just been forcibly removed from office and brought back as a prisoner, could not help remarking bitterly: "Now even the tailors clamor for an opportunity to make discoveries. It is certain that they go for plunder and this they are permitted to do."[13] Less than three years later, the situation had changed. The causes were the failure of Hojeda's second expedition and of Columbus' last voyage, the meager returns, the growing hostility of the Indians, malaria, scurvy, and the mosquitoes. There was less thirst for gold, fewer dreams of getting rich quick. The enthusiasm of the early days was gone. At the beginning of 1504, the Catholic Sovereigns had to resort to heralds and town criers, in Seville, Cadiz, Sanlúcar, Puerto de Santa Maria, to publicize the fact that they would welcome applications for licenses to discover.[14]

If unauthorized expeditions took place, it must have been between 1500 and 1502, and there cannot have been many of them; for they required investments that few individuals could provide, and it was very hard to keep them secret because of the tight controls imposed by the Crown. Of course, the organizers of these clandestine voyages probably enjoyed the connivance of the local authorities who, keeping their eyes closed and their hands open, expected a cut in the profits.

Several historians have mentioned Francisco de Riberol and Juan Sánchez as the promoters of one of those clandestine expeditions, because an order for their arrest was signed by the King and Queen on 4 February 1500. Riberol and Sánchez were accused of dispatching two caravels from Sanlúcar de Barrameda; but in the order for their arrest no mention is made of the destination of the two vessels. It seems that they were headed for Hispaniola with a cargo of merchandise, not for South America. If Riberol and Sánchez were not authorized to trade in the Indies, it was because they were not subjects of Castile, the former being from Genoa, the latter from Aragon. After the Queen's death, Fernando gave Sánchez special permission to do business in Hispaniola.[15]

We shall conclude this discussion by answering the following question: Was there any poaching on the part of foreign nations? The Portuguese did sometimes encroach on Spanish territory west of the demarcation line. We have seen that in 1503 rumors were circulating in Spain that Portuguese ships had gone to the land discovered by Bastidas the year before, and had brought back brazilwood and slaves. La Cosa had been sent to Lisbon to check on such rumors; but his presence there angered the Lusitanian monarch who had him kept in jail for a few weeks.[16]

As for the English, letters from the Spanish ambassadors in London had caused much alarm, because they reported that John Cabot was planning to sail down south from the "New Found Land" he had discovered in 1497; but Cabot disappeared in his next expedition (1498), and the Bristol *Company of Adventurers* who took over after his death seems to have confined its activities to Newfoundland and adjacent lands (Cape Breton and Labrador). It is true that in the Household Books of King Henry VII, there is an entry for rewarding some Portuguese who brought popinjays (parrots) and wildcats to London, and no parrots are to be found in Newfoundland; but since these parrots were brought by Portuguese, they must have come from Brazil.[17]

Appendix

Amerigo Vespucci's Portuguese Voyage

We cannot conclude our study of the Andalusian Voyages without reviewing Amerigo Vespucci's participation in the discovery of South America. We have seen that in his first voyage, the Florentine had sailed with Hojeda in 1499; but when the expedition had come within sight of the north shore of South America at the end of June, Vespucci had parted company with his chief and had sailed southeastward, "since it was my intention to see whether I could turn a headland that Ptolemy calls Cape of Cattigara, which connects with the Sinus Magnus. In my opinion, we were not a great distance from it, according to computed longitude and latitude . . ."[1] So he had pointed his prows toward the southeast, had crossed the equator, had discovered the estuaries of the Amazon and the Para, following the coast until he had been stopped by the adverse South Equatorial Current at a latitude of about 3° south, before reaching his goal. Then he had turned back, caught up with Hojeda, and had returned with him to Spain in June 1500.

Back in Seville, Amerigo revived his aborted project and tried to win the approval of the Catholic Sovereigns. He gave Isabel some of his finest pearls and precious stones, and Fernando, for whom he had made a globe not long before, seemed willing to help. He wrote to Lorenzo di Medici on 18 July: "The King is fitting out for me three ships that I may go again to discover. I believe they will be ready by the middle of September."[2] What was this expedition the Florentine planned to sail with?

Two fleets were then being made ready in Seville for discovery. They were to be led respectively by Rodrigo de Bastidas and Vélez de Mendoza, who had been granted almost identical capitulations on 5 June. La Cosa had agreed to serve with Bastidas as chief pilot; their armada was to sail westward beyond Coquibacoa. The other was being outfitted by Vélez de Mendoza and Luis Guerra, each of whom had provided a caravel. Although we have no proof of it, it seems that Vespucci contacted them and offered his services as chief pilot. He may have also offered a third vessel, hence the reference to "three ships" in his letter to Lorenzo. Soon afterward, toward the end of July, or early in August, Diego de Lepe returned to Spain from his voyage of discovery. He had sailed southwestward, had explored the Brazilian elbow, and had reached Cape Santo Agostinho. In Seville he reported his discovery of the cape, and since he had rounded it and sailed a few leagues beyond, he added that south of the cape the coast stretched endlessly as far as the eye could see. Vespucci must have been delighted with such news, for this was the route he planned to follow to reach Cattigara and then India. "I hope to bring back very great news and discover the island of Taprobana which is in the Indian Ocean, and the Gulf or Sea of Ganges."[3]

Unfortunately for him, events took an unexpected turn. On 18 August Vélez de Mendoza received orders forbidding him to admit foreigners in his expedition. This measure left Vespucci out and must have been directed against him, for Vélez's original capitulation contained no such prohibition. Why this sudden *coup de théâtre?* Fernando and Isabel probably decided that it was not safe to let a foreigner learn "the secrets" of lands they considered their own, for it was not yet known in Spain that Cape Santo Agostinho and the coast south of it fell within the zone assigned to Portugal by the treaty of Tordesillas. As a matter of fact, Alvares Cabral had already taken possession of it for Portugal in April 1500 on his way to Cape of Good Hope and India.

Moreover, on the same day (18 August) and in another additional clause to his capitulation, Vélez was required to have his sailing charts checked and to follow the route that would be traced for him. Since this route led to Cape Santo Agostinho and beyond, Vélez could have no better guide than Bartolomé Roldán, Lepe's pilot, one of the ablest and most experienced seamen in Spain, who had just returned from Cape Santo Agostinho and was familiar with the route the armada was to follow. And as a faithful subject of their Catholic Majesties, Roldán could be depended up to keep quiet and reveal no "secrets;" while it was felt that a skilled, wealthy, and ambitious foreigner like Vespucci, who wrote long letters to influential friends abroad in which he reported *his* discoveries, could imperil national security.

The Vélez expedition sailed toward the end of August, with Bartolomé Roldán as chief pilot. It was gone nine and a half months, reached Cape Santo Agostinho, and kept sailing beyond, along the Brazilian seaboard. How far south did it go? We know that it captured native slaves in a country called *Topia* (Land of the Tupi Indians), and that it was anchored on Christmas Day 1500 at the mouth of a river that its leaders baptized *Río de Cervatos* (Fawn or Deer River). In a previous chapter, we suggested that the Rio de Cervatos might be the São Francisco River, but this is merely a guess. During the nine and a half months that their voyage lasted, Vélez and Luis Guerra could have sailed far down the coast, even beyond Porto Seguro (16° S.) where Alvares Cabral had struck land some six months earlier. During the first *Pleitos de Colón* (1512–1513), some pilots testified that Alonso Vélez and Luis Guerra "discovered from *Cape Cruz* (Cape Santo Agostinho) toward the south all that is discovered now."[4] If we take this assertion literally, it would imply that the Vélez–Guerra expedition discovered the Rio de la Plata and reached it one year before Amerigo Vespucci.

As for the Florentine, the departure of the Vélez armada had left him stranded in Seville, but not for long. According to his own testimony he was summoned to Lisbon by King Manoel to take part in an expedition of discovery which was being sent to the east coast of Brazil to follow up the land strike made in April 1500 by Alvares Cabral at Porto Seguro. This was precisely the coast that Amerigo had hoped to explore for Spain. The three ships with which he sailed left Lisbon on 13 May 1501. We know nothing about that fleet and who commanded it, since the arrogant Florentine, in his usual manner, mentions no one but himself, always speaks in the first person, and gives himself all the credit. The armada stopped over at Cabo Verde, where it met two of Cabral's ships returning from India. Through them, Amerigo learned more about the Portuguese discovery of Brazil the year before, and he made the following comment: "This was the same land which I discovered for the King of Castile, . . . only their land-fall was farther in the East."[5]

After leaving Cabo Verde, Amerigo and his companions sailed south-southwest for 64 days until they struck land in the vicinity of Cape São Roque, and they followed the east coast of Brazil for 800 leagues, reaching the latitude of 40° S in Patagonia. They spent several months below the equator without seeing the North Pole and the Dippers. Amerigo did not spend all his time at sea, for he was eager to study the natives' way of life. "For twenty-seven days I ate and slept among them." As they sailed down the coast, he and his companions baptized various landmarks with the names of saints whose day it was when a cape, a bay, or the mouth of a river was being discovered. For example: Cape São Roque (5°S.) 14 August; Cape Santo Agostinho (8°S.) 28 August; São Francisco River (10°S.) 4 October; All Saints Bay (13°S.) 1 November. At the latitude of 25°S., the coast, which had been running south-southwest, crossed the demarcation line and reentered the Spanish zone. Ten degrees farther south, they reached a huge estuary and called it *Rio Jordam* (today Rio de La Plata).

We don't know the exact date of their return to Lisbon, since Amerigo's letter to Lorenzo is undated. It may have been 22 July 1502.[6] The tone of that letter shows an evolution in his thinking. To be sure he mentions having discovered a new land, which he thinks is a landmass (*terra ferma*), using the same terms as did Columbus in 1498 to announce his discovery of Paria, and he also alludes to similarities with the Earthly Paradise. But what he leaves out of his letter is far more significant than what he wrote. He probably had hoped to find Cattigara at 9° S. as in Ptolemy, or in the vicinity of the Tropic of Capricorn at 23° S. as in Behaim or Martellus (actually the Malacca Peninsula is 1° north); but he had sailed as far as 40° south without finding it. As for Taprobana and the Ganges, he had learned at Cabo Verde that Alvares Cabral had already beaten him to them. By checking longitudes, he must have realized that the coast he had just explored was still far from China and India. He no longer thought of discovery, but of working out a scheme for the exploitation of the new lands.

When they reached Lisbon, Amerigo and his companions must have compared notes with the pilots of the Cabral armada. The result of their consultations was the concoction of maps of the Cantino-Canerio type, which pictured South America as a shapeless landmass without any connection with Asia. Its contours were outlined in the north and the east, but were left undefined in the south and in the west. On those maps, the islands discovered by Columbus during his first and second voyages were called "The Antillas of the King of Spain," being identified with the legendary archipelago of Antilla; but Cuba, largest of the group, was duplicated and appeared twice, as an island called *Isabela,* and as a landmass named *Tierra de Cuba,* because of the confusion originated by Columbus, who, after calling Cuba an island, changed his mind and decided that it was part of the Asiatic mainland.[7]

Lisbon was then a hotbed of new geographical concepts forcing navigators and mapmakers to revise their views. In this environment, Vespucci and others conceived the new antipodal *tierra firme* as a continent independent of the traditional tripartite world of the Bible and Ptolemy. This concept soon found its way to other countries, through letters and other writings attributed rightly or wrongly to Amerigo, and addressed to friends in Florence and to Duke René of Lorraine. In the small town of Saint-Dié, at the foot of the Vosges mountains, a local schoolteacher called Martin Waldseemüller designed a world map on which the southern continent was labeled *America* (1507), giving Vespucci all the credit for its discovery.[8]

Yet others had participated in the exploration of the new *tierra firme* and had reached the same conclusion, that it was independent of Asia. One of them was Duarte Pacheco Pereira, a well-known Portuguese navigator and geographer. He had sailed with Alvares Cabral's armada, had witnessed the land strike made at Porto Seguro on the east coast of Brazil (April 1500), had gone to India, and had returned in the summer of 1501. Two years later, he sailed back to the Orient with Albuquerque, distinguished himself as a soldier and statesman, and returned in 1504. During the following year he wrote the initial chapters of his work *Esmeraldo de situ orbis,* in which he went much further than Vespucci and Waldseemüller, who limited the new continent to South America, and included in it the lands already discovered in the North Atlantic (Cape Breton, Newfoundland, Labrador). He thus conceived a continent stretching vertically from pole to pole and forming a barrier between Europe and East Asia.

"A very large landmass with many islands adjacent, extending 70 degrees north of the equator, and located beyond the greatness of the ocean, has been discovered and navigated. This distant land is densely populated and extends 28 and half degrees on the other side of the equator towards the Antarctic Pole. Such is its greatness and length that on either side its end has not been seen and known, so that it is certain that it goes around the whole globe."[9]

This new conception of a whole western hemisphere was at first completely ignored. It became accepted by cartographers only after 1520 when the exploration of the American coastline was completed. Two expeditions were sent in 1523 and 1524, one by France (led by Giovanni Verrazano), and the other by Spain (led by Esteban Gómez), in final attempts to find a northwest passage to the Moluccas. Both followed the shore from Florida to Nova Scotia. They searched in vain for the passage; instead, they found a continuous coastline. The earliest map to show the Atlantic side of the Western Hemisphere complete from head to foot, from Labrador to Tierra del Fuego (except for Yucatan, which was still believed by some to be an island) was a world map drawn by Diogo Ribeiro in 1525, after the return of Esteban Gómez to Spain (21 August 1525). The latter had discovered a land which stretched from the Hudson to Maine and filled the last gap on previous maps. This land became known as the *Tierra de Esteban Gómez*.[10]

If Pacheco seems to have conceived South America as distinct from Asia at about the same time as Vespucci, he was certainly the first to realize the existence of a western continent including lands as far north as Labrador. Therefore, we may wonder if *America la bien llamada* (the well named), as a Latin American historian calls it, would not have been more appropriately named *Eduarda* or *Pacheca;* but, everything considered, *America* sounds better.

Amerigo did not stay long in Lisbon, for he had there another taste of the ungratefulness of kings. The Lusitanian monarch Dom Manoel "the well served" did not reward him for his services. Amerigo entrusted to him a detailed account of his 1501 voyage. The King was supposed to return it, but we have no proof that he ever did. The Florentine also submitted a plan for the economic exploitation of the new land, but he was passed over in favor of some Portuguese *conversos*.[11] Disgusted, he left Portugal and went back to Seville (October 1502), to try again his luck in Spain. He had a trump card, because he had found out that the east coast of South America crossed the partition line at a latitude of 25° S. so that the southern part of the new continent could be claimed for Spain.

Vespucci and Columbus became good friends and sympathized with each other since both felt they had been unjustly treated. From a letter of the Genoese to his son Diego, we learn that Amerigo was trying to ingratiate himself at the Court and was eager to serve.[12] He did succeed, and his merits were finally recognized in 1505, when he was granted Spanish citizenship and appointed pilot of the House of Trade, being promoted later to *piloto mayor*. He died in Spain in 1512 highly considered by his fellow cosmographers.

Abbreviations

MANUSCRIPT MATERIAL

AGI	Archivo General de Indias
AGS	Archivo General de Simancas
AMS	Archivo Municipal, de Sevilla
APS	Archivo de Protocolos de Sevilla

PRINTED MATERIAL

CDIAO   *Colección de documentos inéditos relativos al descubrimiento, conquista y organisación de las antiguas posesiones españolas de América y Oceania,* 42 vols. (Madrid, 1864–84).

CDIU   *Colección de documentos inéditos relativos al descubrimiento, conquista y organisación de las antiguas posesiones españolas de Ultramar,* 25 vols. (Madrid, 1885–1932).

Las Casas   Bartolomé de las Casas, *Historia de las Indias,* ed. Agustín Millares Carlo, 3 vols. (Mexico City, 1951).

Navarrete   Martín Fernández de Navarrete, *Colección de los viajes y descubrimientos que hicieron por mar los españoles desde el siglo XV,* 5 vols. (Madrid, 1825–39).

Oviedo   Gonzalo Fernández de Oviedo y Valdés, *Historia General y Natural de las Indias,* ed. Juan Pérez de Tudela Bueso, in *Biblioteca de Autores Españoles,* vol. 117–21 (Madrid, 1959).

Pietro Martire   Pietro Martire d'Anghiera, *De Orbe Novo,* tr. from the Latin by Francis Augustus McNutt (New York, 1912).

Raccolta Colombiana   *Raccolta di documenti e studi pubblicati della R. Commissione colombiana, pel cuarto centenario della scoperta dell'America,* 14 vols. (Rome, 1892–96).

NOTES

1 The Discovery of South America by Columbus

1. Henry Vignaud, *Toscanelli and Columbus* (London, 1902). E. G. Ravenstein, *Martin Behaim, His Life and His Globe* (London, 1908), 77.

2. P. Martire d'Anghiera, *De Orbe Novo,* transl. F. A. McNutt (New York, 1912), I, 61. In Biblical times, Ophir was an oriental land from which Solomon obtained gold, precious stones, sandalwood, and ivory to adorn the Temple of Jerusalem (3rd Book of Kings). In medieval geography, Ophir was a mythical island located somewhere in the Indian Ocean. Behaim put it south of the Ganges (Ravenstein, 94).

3. *Raccolta Colombiana* (Rome, 1892), III, i, 166.

4. S. E. Morison, *Admiral of the Ocean Sea* (New York, 1942), II, 141–43.

5. S. E. Morison, *Journals and Other Documents* (New York, 1963), 117. *Raccolta Colombiana,* III, ii, 7.

6. APS, Oficio III, Libro de 1497, fol. 43, 198, 712.

7. Navarrete, *Colección de Viajes* ... (Madrid, 1825), II, 181, 185.

8. Navarrete, II, 207, 209, 212.

9. Navarrete, II, 219.

10. AGI, *Contratación* 3249, fol. 144v.

11. Wine bought at the winery cost 20 maravedis per *arroba* (8 *azumbres* or 4 gallons). Transportation to port of embarkation cost 10 maravedis, the cask 8, transportation across the ocean 50, and *averia* (insurance) 2. Total 90 maravedis (CDIAO, XXX, 472). Since Mariño was expected to sell the *arroba* 120 maravedis (15 per *azumbre*) in Santo Domingo, his profit would be 30 maravedis per *arroba.*

12. AGI, *Contratación,* 3249, fol. 184.

13. AGI, *Contratación,* 3249, 186.

14. Claudius Ptolemy, *Geographia,* transl. E. L. Stevenson (New York, 1932).

15. *Archivo dos Açores,* XII (1892), 388.

16. J. A. Williamson, *The Cabot Voyages and Bristol Discovery under Henry VII* (London: 1962), 201 ff.

17. Duarte Pacheco Pereira, *Esmeraldo de Situ Orbis* (London, 1937), 12.

18. Williamson, 228.

19. APS, Oficio XV, Libro de 1501, fol. 227v–228.

20. AGS, *Cédulas de Camara,* Libro IV, fol. 252.

21. A. A. Ruddock, "John Day of Bristol and the English voyages across the Atlantic before 1497," *Geographical Journal*, vol. 132 (1966), 225–33.

22. L.-A. Vigneras, "The Cape Breton Landfall: 1494 Or 1497. Note on a letter from John Day," *Canadian Historical Review*, vol. 38 (1957), 219–29. The translation of Day's letter has been reprinted in Williamson, 211–14.

23. Navarrete, II, 105. Morison, *Admiral*, II, 233–34.

24. For a detailed account of this voyage, see Morison, *Admiral*, II, 232–74.

25. Morison, *Admiral*, 274–93.

26. Morison, *Admiral*, 294–302.

27. His secretary, Bernaldo de Ibarra, who later became a good friend of Bartolomé de las Casas, probably gave him copies of the said letters, for he quotes from them in his *Historia de las Indias*, ed. Millares Carlo (Mexico City, 1951), II, 12 ff.

28. For a translation of the letter, see Morison, *Journals*, 284–88.

29. Edmundo O'Gorman, *La Idea del Descubrimiento de América* (Mexico City, 1951).

30. W. Washburn, "The Meaning of Discovery," *American Historical Review*, vol. 68 (October 1962), 1–21.

31. This world map is part of an atlas of eight maps by Andrea Bianco preserved in the Biblioteca Marciana in Venice.

32. Pierre d'Ailly, *Imago Mundi*, ed. and transl. Edmond Buron (Paris, 1930), 198. Chapter 56 (p. 468 ff.) is devoted to the rivers of Paradise.

33. *Pleitos de Colón*, in CDIU, vol. 7 and 8. The University of Seville has undertaken a complete edition of the *Pleitos*, but so far only vols. I and VIII have come out.

2 The Business of Discovery

1. Navarrete, III, 85.

2. Navarrete, III, 80.

3. Vicente Yañez Pinzón (6 June 1499), *Anuario de Estudios Americanos*, IV, 745 ss.
Alonso Vélez de Mendoza (5 June 1500), AGS, *Libro de cédulas* IV, fol. 103–4. Unpublished.
Rodrigo de Bastidas (5 June 1500), Navarrete, II, 244–46.
Alonso de Hojeda (end of May 1501), Navarrete, III, 85.
Vicente Yañez Pinzón (5 September 1501), CDIAO, XXX, 535–42.
Diego de Lepe (14 September 1501), CDIAO, XXXI, 5–12.
Juan de Escalante (5 October 1501), CDIAO, XXXI, 90–95.
Juan de la Cosa ⎫
Cristóbal Guerra ⎬ (14 February 1504), CDIAO, XXXI, 220–29.
Rodrigo de Bastidas ⎭
Alonso de Hojeda (30 September 1504), CDIAO, XXXI, 258 ff.

4. Navarrete, II, 247–51. This revised version must not be confused with the original capitulation, which has never been published. See note above.

5. Navarrete, III, 85.

6. *Anuario de Estudios Americanos,* IV, 747.

7. See page 61.

8. *Tumbo de los Reyes Católicos,* ed. Juan de Mata Carriazo (Seville, 1968) IV, 311.

9. See page 98.

10. CDIAO, XXXI, 196.

11. P. Martire, I, 164–65.

12. Navarrete, III, 82.

13. AGI, *Contratación* 4674, Primer Libro Manual fol. 46v.

14. AGI, *Ibid.,* fol. 39.

15. AGI, *Ibid.,* fol. 42.

16. *Siete Partidas,* Ley 9, Tit. XIII, Partida I.

17. Edouard Wittevroughel, *De Nautico Foenore* (Dunkerque, 1895), 3–14.

18. Vallés y Pujals, *Del Prestamo a interés* (Barcelona, 1933), 53–65.

19. Cristóbal de Villalón, *Provechoso tratado de cambios y contratación de mercaderes* (Valladolid, 1546), 28–29.

20. APS, Oficio V, Libro de 1500, fol. 287.

21. APS, Oficio V, Libro de 1500, fol. 303.

22. George O'Brien, *Essay on Medieval Economic Teaching* (London, 1920), 205–12. Frederick E. Flynn, *Wealth and Money in the Economic Philosophy of St. Thomas* (Notre Dame, Ind., 1942). Tomas de Mercado, *Summa de tratos y contratos* (Sevilla, 1571), 48–55. Doctor Sarabia de la Calle, *Instrucción de mercaderes* (Medina del Campo, 1544). Reprint (Madrid, 1949), 118–19.

23. APS, Oficio IV, Libro de 1496 a 1498, fol. 235.

24. APS, Oficio IV, Libro II de 1501, fol. 337v–338.

25. Navarrete, III, 91.

26. *Catálogo de los Fondos Americanos del Archivo de Protocolos de Sevilla,* I (Madrid, 1930), 446–47.

27. APS, Oficio IV, Libro I de 1501, fol. 131–33.

28. APS, Oficio V, Libro II de 1504, fol. 388–90.

29. Williamson, 125 ff.

30. Navarrete, I, 411–21.

31. Quirino de Fonseca, *A Caravela Portuguesa* (Coimbra, 1934), 140–51. Morison, *Admiral,* I, xxxvi–xli.

32. J. M. Martínez-Hidalgo, *Columbus' Ships* (Barre, Mass, 1966), 97. Morison, *Admiral,* I, 150–54.

33. Morison, *Journals,* 280–81.

34. Navarrete, II, 293.

35. Frederick C. Lane, *Venice and History* (Baltimore, 1966), 362. Martinez-Hidalgo, 40.

36. Morison, *Admiral*, I, 153–54.

37. Martínez-Hidalgo, 63.

38. See table, page 95.

39. AGI, *Indiferente General* 418, Registro 3, fol. 90–93.

40. Hieronymus Monetarius (Münzer), "Itinerarium Hispanicum," ed. Ludwig Pfandl, *Revue Hispanique*, vol. 48 (1920), 79.

41. For a detailed study, see E. J. Hamilton, 152–78.

42. James Boyd Thacher. *Christopher Columbus* (N.Y., 1902), I, 484–90. Morison, *Admiral*, I, xiii.

43. AGI *Contratación* 4674. Primer Libro Manual, fol. 93–94.

44. Ramón Carande y Tovar, *Carlos V y sus banqueros* (Madrid. 1943), I, 135–42. James Vicens Vives, *An Economic History of Spain* (Princeton, 1969), 309–10. Earl J. Hamilton, *American Treasure and the Price Revolution in Spain* (Cambridge, Mass., 1934), 46–52.

3 The Andalusian Voyages

1 Hojeda, La Cosa, and Vespucci

1. L.-A. Vigneras, "Antecedentes familiares de Alonso de Hojeda," *Revista de Indias*, nos. 130–31 (1973). See also note 22.

2. The Chirinos were *conversos*, that is, Jewish converts to Christianity.

3. *Pleitos de Colón*, CDIU, VII, 313–14 (testimony of Pedro de Soria).

4. APS, Oficio V, Libro de 1500, fol. 48v.

5. Information against Hojeda made by order of Christopher Columbus (June 1500), published by the Duquesa de Berwick y de Alba, *Autógrafos de Cristóbal Colón y Papeles de América* (Madrid, 1892), 27.

6. *Pleitos de Colón*, CDIU, VIII, 205.

7. For Italian text of the letter, see Alberto Magnaghi, *Amerigo Vespucci* (Rome, 1926), 235–45. An English translation will be found in Frederick Julius Pohl, *Amerigo Vespucci* (London, 1966), 76–90.

8. F. J. Pohl, 77.

9. In a 1502 document, Hojeda referred to the losses he had suffered in that battle (Navarrete, III, 105).

10. Pohl, 84.

11. Pohl, 85–86.

12. Pohl, 86.

13. Las Casas, II, 136.

14. Duquesa de Berwick y Alba, 25–38.

15. Las Casas, II, 142.
16. Las Casas, II, 37.
17. *Pleitos de Colón,* CDIU, VII, 102.
18. CDIU, VII, 294, 298.
19. Pohl, 77.
20. Las Casas, II, 140.
21. Pohl, 88.
22. APS, Oficio IV, Libro II de 1500, fol. 430.
23. Pohl, 128.
24. See page 88.

2 Peralonso Niño and Cristóbal Guerra

1. AGI, *Contratación* 3249, fol. 192v.
2. CDIU, VII, 181.
3. Las Casas, II, 146.
4. Martire, I, 155.
5. Martire, I, 167 ff.
6. Martire, I, 156–57.
7. Martire, I, 156.
   Las Casas, II ,149.
8. Navarrete, III, 78.

3 Vicente Yañez Pinzón

1. Navarrete, III, 75.
2. *Anuario de Estudios Americanos,* IV, 745–58.
3. *Pleitos,* CDIU, VIII, 202.
4. P. Martire, I, 158. But Angelo Trevisan (*Libretto de tutta la Navigatione de Re de Spagna,* Paris, 1929, fol. D ii) and Francesco Montalboddo (*Paesi novamente ritrovati,* Princeton, 1916, p. 126) change the date of Yañez's departure to November 18. Martire is our best source for this voyage.
5. Navarrete, I, 256–57.
6. According to E. Roukema ("Some remarks on the La Cosa Map," *Imago Mundi,* XIV, 38–54), Pinzón's *Cabo de la Consolación* was Cape Orange, on the Guyana coast. I find it hard to believe, because the distance between Cape Orange and Paria falls far short from the 600 to 800 leagues Yañez is credited with by the sources.
7. Martire, I, 162–63.
8. Navarrete, I, 267. *Pleitos de Colón,* CDIU, VIII, 51.
9. Las Casas, II, 157–58. Martire, I, 165.
10. Navarrete, III, 82.

11. Navarrete II, 406.

12. CDIAO, XXX, 535–36.

13. Navarrete, III ,79.

14. CDIU, VIII, 140, 225 (testimonies of Juan de Umbria and Arias Pérez).

15. CDIU, VII, 268 (testimony of Yañez Pinzón).

4 Diego de Lepe

1. Las Casas, II, 158.

2. Navarrete, III, 145–46. According to Angel Ortega (*La Rábida,* Seville, 1925, II, 324) Lepe was Martín Alonso's and Vicente Yañez's brother-in-law.

3. Thacher, I, 479.

4. *Pleitos,* CDIU, VIII, 132, 198 (testimonies of Alonso Rodríguez de la Calva and Cristóbal García).

5. Las Casas, II, 159.

6. *Pleitos,* CDIU, VII, 299.

7. APS, Oficio V, Libro de 1501, fol. 72 (loose leaf).

8. Navarrete, II, 247.

9. Navarrete, III, 80.

10. Letter from the Sovereigns, Navarrete, III, 81. Capitulation, CDIAO, XXXI, 5–12.

11. AGI, *Indiferente General* 418, I, fol. 64v.

12. AGI, *Indiferente General* 418, I, fol. 69v–70.

13. APS, Oficio XV, Libro de 1501, fol. 724, 745v.

14. APS, Oficio IV, Libro I de 1501, fol. 131–33.

15. AGI, *Indiferente General,* 418, I, 77v.

16. *Pleitos,* CDIU, VII, 202.

17. CDIAO, XXXI, 90–95.

18. AGI, *Indiferente General* 418, I, 70v–71.

19. *Pleitos,* CDIU, VIII, 82.

20. *Archivo dos Açores,* XII, 387, 398, 405–6.

5 Alonso Vélez de Mendoza and Luis Guerra

1. The capitulation of Vélez de Mendoza has never been published. The only extant copy is in Simancas (AGS, *Cédulas de Camara* IV, fol. 103).

2. APS, Oficio V, Libro I (1441–1504), fol. 20.

3. APS, Oficio V, Libro de 1500, fol. 77. This register, which had been missing for thirty years, was rediscovered in 1972.

4. APS, Oficio V, Libro de 1500, fol. 238.

5. Joannes Duns Scotus, *Commentaria Oxoniensa ad IV libros Magistri Sentenciarum* (Quaracchi-Florence, 1914), II, 594–600. The question for discussion is "Whether Paradise is a place fit for human living."

6. AGI, *Contratación* 3249, fol. 16.

7. AMS, *Mayordomazgo,* 30 de Agosto 1493.

8. APS, Oficio V, Libro de 1500, fol. 14 (10 January), 273 (10 May), and two loose leaves dated 1 June.

9. APS, Oficio IV, Libro de 1495, fol. 28.

10. APS, Oficio V, Libro de 1500, fol. 284v–85v.

11. APS, Oficio V, Libro de 1500, fol. 297v–98v.

12. APS, Oficio V, Libro de 1500, fol. 286.

13. APS, Oficio V, Libro de 1500, fol. 287, 303.

14. AMS, *Mayordomazgo,* 1483–84.

15. J. Gestoso y Pérez, *Sevilla Monumental y Artística,* 3 vols. (Seville, 1889–92), I, 185.

16. APS, Oficio IV, Libro de 1500, fol. 541.

17. See the will of Costancia Rodríguez Tiscareño (2 September 1501), APS, Oficio IV, Libro II de 1501, fol. 176. The name Tiscareño appears on lists of comitres as early as 1436. Two of Cristóbal's brothers were members of the Brotherhood.

18. Navarrete, II, 247. This revised version must not be confused with the original capitulation. See note 1.

19. *Pleitos,* CDIU, VII, 195, 202–3, 221, 304; VIII, 226–27.

20. J. T. Medina *El veneciano Sebastián Caboto al servicio de España* (2 vols., Santiago de Chile, 1908), I, 500.

21. APS, Oficio XV, Libro de 1501, fol. 417v–18.

22. APS, Oficio XV, Libro de 1501, fol. 306–9. The "Río de Cervatos" is mentioned three times. For helping me decipher the name, I am indebted to friends in the Archivo de Indias and the University of Seville.

23. APS, Oficio IV, Libro I de 1501, fol. 279v–80.

24. APS, Oficio XV, Libro de 1501, fol. 306–9.

25. APS, Oficio IV, Libro I de 1501, fol. 291v–92.

26. APS, Oficio XV, Libro de 1501, fol. 299v–300, 306–9.

27. APS, Oficio III, Libro de 1501, fol. 458–61.

28. APS, Oficio XV, Libro de 1501, fol. 417v–18.

29. APS, Oficio XV, Libro de 1501, fol. 400–1.

30. APS, Oficio IV, Libro I de 1501, fol. 447.

31. APS, Oficio IV, Libro II de 1501, fol. 103v.

32. APS, Oficio IV, Libro II de 1501, fol. 216v–17.

33. APS, Oficio IV, Libro I de 1501, fol. 145–46. In a census of prisoners kept in the Seville jail at the end of March 1502 (APS, Oficio IV, Libro I de 1502), Vélez is still listed. His name is last on the list and seems to have been added on second thought. Apparently he was enjoying almost complete freedom, but he had not yet settled all his debts.

34. CDIAO XXXI, 121–29.

35. Ortega, II, 318–19.

36. Ortega, II, 327–28. AGI, *Contratación* 5575, no. I. This list was originally thought to be the list of the 37 men Columbus had left in Hispaniola in January 1493.

37. *Catálogo de Fondos Americanos,* I, no. 36.

6 Cristóbal Guerra and Diego de Grajeda

1. AGS, *Estado* I, Parte II, fol. 158.

2. AGI, *Contratación* 4674, Libro III, 1507.

3. ". . . y en el segundo viaje, llevé una caravela de cincuenta toneladas, que era la de Grajeda," letter of Cristóbal Guerra to Don Alvaro de Portugal, Navarrete, II, 293.

4. Juan de Noya testified in the *Pleitos* (CDIU, VII, 255) that he took part in Cristóbal's second voyage. Pero de la Puebla is mentioned as pilot of Cristóbal's caravel in APS, Oficio III, Libro de 1501, fol. 569. Alice Gould cites Francisco Gálvez as master of the said caravel (*Boletín de la Academia de la Historia,* Tomo CX, 153, n. 2); but she does not give her source. Since Miss Gould's name is a guarantee of sound scholarship, I am willing to accept Gálvez as master of Guerra's caravel, even though I have been unable to check her statement.

5. APS, Oficio V, Libro de 1502–3, fol. 57v–58.

6. APS, Oficio IV, Libro II de 1501, fol. 337v–38.

7. Boletín, 153, n. 2. For the text of Cantino's letter, see *Raccolta Colombiana,* III, i, 152.

8. The cassia fistula is the drumstick tree. See Sterling A. Stoudemire's translation of Oviedo's *Natural History,* 9, 19.

9. AGI, *Indiferente General* 418, Libro I, fol. 68.

10. AGI, *Ibid.,* fol. 70, 72v–75.

11. AGI, *Ibid.,* fol. 114. CDIU, V, 63.

12. L.-A. Vigneras, "El Viaje de Esteban Gómez a Norte América," *Revista de Indias,* vol. 17 (1957), 198.

7 Rodrigo de Bastidas and Juan de la Cosa

1. Navarrete, II, 244–46.

2. J. Real Diaz, "El Sevillano Rodrigo de Bastidas," *Archivo Hispalense,* Nos. 111–12 (1962), 61 ff.

3. *Catálogo de Fondos Americanos,* I, 445–51.

4. AGI, *Indiferente General* 418, Registro III, fol. 90–93.

5. *Pleitos,* CDIU, VII, 210. This means that Bastidas' capitulation like Vélez de Mendoza's, was modified to exclude foreigners.

6. Las Casas, II, 408.

7. APS, Oficio III, Libro de 1501, fol. 84–85.

8. Gerardo Reichel-Dolmatoff, *Colombia* (New York, 1965), 142–58.

9. *Handbook of South American Indians,* IV (New York, 1963), 330–38. B. Le Roy Gordon, *Human Geography and Ecology in the Sinu Country of Colombia* (Berkeley, 1957). Reichel-Dolmatoff, 125–28. See also Martín Fernández de Enciso's description of the coast from Cabo de la Vela to Darien, in his *Suma de Geografía* (1518), reprinted in Madrid (1948), 214–22. There is an English translation by Roger Barlow, edited by E. G. R. Taylor (Hakluyt, Ser. II, vol. 69), but it is not complete.

10. A. Bernáldez, *Historia de los Reyes Católicos,* Biblioteca de autores Españoles, LXX (Madrid, 1878), 718.

11. Navarrete, II, 414–16. CDIAO, XXXI, 196.

12. Las Casas, II, 411.

13. James J. Parsons, "Santa Maria la Antigua del Darien," *Geographical Review,* vol. 50 (1960), 294–96.

14. Las Casas, II, 210.

15. *Pleitos,* CDIU, VII, 213. Testimony of Juan de Quicedo (or Quecedo).

16. The remark above is from S. E. Morison (*Journals,* 355, n. 2) and refers to Columbus' fourth and last voyage; but it applies as well to Bastidas in 1501. Furthermore, La Cosa had a similar experience in 1505.

17. Navarrete, II, 416.

18. Bernáldez, 718.

19. Navarrete, II, 419–20.

20. AGI, *Indiferente General* 418, Libro III, 90, 91. Juan de Grado who had invested 13,500 maravedis, received 14,850. Diego Hurtado was paid 24,200 maravedis for an investment of 22,000. We don't have individual figures for the other *compañeros,* but the dividend they received must have been the same.

21. AGI, *Contratación* 4674, Primer Libro Manual, fol. 45v, 46v.

22. CDIAO, XXXI, 230.

23. CDIAO, XXXI, 129–31.

24. Bernáldez, 719.

25. AGI, *Contratación* 4674, Primer Libro Manual, fol. 23. AGI, *Indiferente General* 418, Libro I, 104. La Cosa's captivity in Lisbon is mentioned by Cristóbal Guerra in his letter to Don Alvaro de Portugal (Navarrete, II, 292).

8 Hojeda, Vergara, and Campos

1. Navarrete, III, 85.

2. Navarrete, III, 84.

3. Navarrete, III, 85, 89.

4. Navarrete, III, 91.

5. Navarrete, III, 101.

6. The main source for the history of this voyage is a copious file of documents

dealing with the trial of Alonso de Hojeda in 1503 in Santo Domingo, where his two associates brought him as a prisoner. The trial lasted several months, and many members of the expedition testified for the accusation or for the defense (AGS, *Diversos de Castilla,* Leg. 45, No. 3). Navarrete has published the review of the case and final sentence by the Royal Council (II, 420–36).

7. Navarrete, III, 103.

8. Navarrete, III, 105.

9. Navarrete, III, 106.

10. AGS, *Diversos de Castilla,* 45, no. 3, fol. 25: ". . . estando yo en servicio de sus altezas haciendo una fuerza de tapias en la dicha isla de Coquibacoa, en la provincia que dicen de Paraguana. . . ."

11. *Handbook of South American Indians,* IV, 329–38.

12. Navarrete, III, 107.

13. Testifying eleven years later in the *Pleitos de Colón* (CDIU, VII, 205–6), Hojeda also claimed that from Coquibacoa he had sent the pilot Antón García on a reconnaissance mission, in the course of which García sailed westward, reached Urabá and Darien, and reached the Puerto del Retrete after Bastidas, but before Columbus. This rather questionable statement of Hojeda is not confirmed by any other source. It was probably dictated by his dislike of the Columbus family.

14. AGS, *Diversos de Castilla,* 45, no. 3, fol. 31v.

15. AGS, *Ibid.,* fol. 87v, 169.

16. AGS, *Ibid.,* fol. 192.

17. Navarrete, II, 420–36.

9/10 Cristóbal and Luis Guerra
Juan de la Cosa and Juan de Ledesma

1. Navarrete, II, 414–16.

2. AGI, *Indiferente General* 418, Libro I, 87v–88.

3. CDIAO, XXXI, 187–93.

4. Navarrete, II, 292.

5. A. Ballesteros, *La Marina Cantabra,* 290–93. For a detailed account of La Cosa's 1504–1506 voyage, see pp. 318–44.

6. Navarrete, III, 109.

7. CDIAO, XXXI, 220–29.

8. *Archivo Hispalense,* vol. 111–12 (1962), 61 ff. AGI, *Justicia* 9, No. 1.

9. AGI, *Contratación* 4674, Primer Libro Manual, fol. 29.

10. Oviedo, III, 131–33.

11. Las Casas, II, 152–53.

12. CDIAO, XXXI, 248.

13. APS, Oficio V, Libro II de 1504, fol. 388–90.

14. APS, Oficio IV, Libro de 1504, fol. 701–3.

15. APS, Oficio IV, Libro II de 1504, 324.

16. Oviedo, II, 131.

17. Marino Sanuto, *Diarii* (Venice, 1879), VI, 539–41.

18. Saddened by his brothers' death overseas, Antón Mariño does not seem to have engaged in other voyages of discovery. He probably remained in Seville carrying on the family business. But one of his sons, Diego Guerra, applied for a license to go to America on 2 November 1512 (*Catálogo de pasajeros a Indias*, I, no. 850). Another son, a priest named Luis Guerra, made a contract with Juan de Medina, owner of the *Santa Maria de la Granada* for the shipment of a cargo of merchandise to Santo Domingo in 1520 (APS, Oficio VII, Libro de 1520, fol. 37 of cuaderno 10). After this we lose track of the Guerras of Triana.

19. *Sailing Directions for West Indies*, vol. I, 3rd edition 1958 (H.O. PUB. 21), Pedro Banks and Cays 322–23; Black River Bay 354–55.

20. The *hutia* is a large rodent native to the West Indies, where it is hunted for its flesh.

21. APS, Oficio XI, 13 de Marzo 1506.

22. Oviedo, III, 137.

23. APS, Oficio III, 7 de Abril 1506, fol. 344.

24. AGI, *Contratación* 4674, Primer Libro Manual, fol. 93v–94.

25. AGI, *Ibid.*, fol. 104, 114v.

11   Alonso de Hojeda and Pedro de la Cueva

1. CDIAO, XXXI, 258 ff.

2. AGI, *Indiferente General* 418, Libro I, fol. 138v, 139, 178v.

3. AGI, *Contratación* 4674, Primer Libro Manual, fol. 142. The *cornado* (contraction of *coronado*) was worth one sixth of a maravedi at the time. The 26 maravedis and 4 cornados a day would amount to 800 maravedis a month.

4. AGI, *Indiferente General* 418, Libro I, fol. 139v.

5. APS, Oficio IV, Libro IV de 1509, fol. 2924 ss.

6. AGI, *Indiferente General* 418, Libro I, fol. 151.

7. AGI, *Contratación* 4674, Primer Libro Manual, low. 51v.

8. AGI, *Indiferente General* 418, Libro I, fol. 183.

9. AGI, *Contratación* 4674, Primer Libro Manual, fol. 94, 97v.

10. A. Ortega, *La Rábida*, II, 325–26.

11. *Pleitos*, CDIU, VII, 281–82.

12. AGI, *Indiferente General*, 418, Libro I, fol. 26, 41v. Navarrete, II, 257–59.

13. S. E. Morison, *Journals*, 384.

14. AGI, *Contratación* 4674, Primer Libro Manual, fol. 27v, 30v.

15. Navarrete, III, 513, 525.
16. AGI, *Contratación* 4674, Primer Libro Manual, fol. 23.
    AGI, *Indiferente General* 418, Libro I, 104.
17. J. A. Williamson, 216.

Appendix

1. F. J. Pohl, 77.
2. Pohl, 88–89.
3. Pohl, 89.
4. See Fifth Voyage.
5. Pohl, 128.
6. See letter of Pietro Pasqualigo, *Raccolta Colombiana,* III, i, 91.
7. George E. Nunn, *The Geographical Conceptions of Columbus* (reprinted New York, 1924), 91–140.
8. See map in Martin Waldseemüller, *The Cosmographiae Introductio* (New York, 1907).
9. Duarte Pacheco Pereira, *Esmeraldo de Situ Orbis,* 12–13.
10. L.-A. Vigneras, "The Cartographer Diogo Ribeiro," *Imago Mundi,* XVI (1962), 77–78.
11. Pohl, 145. Magnaghi, 202.
12. Pohl, 162.

Bibliography

Ailly, Pierre d'. *Imago Mundi*. Ed. and transl. Edmond Buron. Paris, 1930.

Alfonso X El Sabio. *Las Siete Partidas*. 4 vols. Ed. Gregorio López. Madrid, 1843–44.

Anghiera, Pietro Martire d'. *De Orbe Novo*. Transl. T. A. McNutt. New York, 1912.

Archivo dos Açores. Vol. XII. Ponta Delgada, 1892.

Babcock, William Henry. *Legendary Islands of the Atlantic*. New York, 1922.

Ballesteros y Beretta, Antonio. *La Marina Cantabra y Juan de la Cosa*. Santander, 1954.

Bernáldez, Andrés. *Historia de los Reyes Católicos*. Biblióteca de autores españoles, LXX. Madrid, 1878.

Berwick y Alba, Duquesa de. *Autógrafos de Cristóbal Colón y Papeles de América*. Madrid, 1892.

Carande y Tovar, Ramón. *Carlos V y sus banqueros*. Madrid, 1943.

Casas, Bartolomé de las. *Historia de las Indias*. 3 vols. Ed. A. Millares Carlos. Mexico City, 1951.

Catálogo de los Fondos Americanos del Archivo de Protocolos de Sevilla. 5 vols. Madrid, 1930, 1932, 1935; Seville, 1937.

Catálogo de Pasajeros a Indias. Vol. I. Seville, 1940.

Columbus, Ferdinand. *The Life of the Admiral Christopher Columbus*. Transl. Benjamin Keen. New Brunswick, 1959.

Duns Scotus, Joannes. *Commentaria Oxoniensa ad IV libros Magistri Sentenciarum*. Quaracchi-Florence, 1914.

Enciso, Martín, Fernández de. *A Brief Summe of Geographie*. Transl. Roger Barlow. Ed. E. G. R. Taylor. London, 1948.

———. *Suma de Geografía*. Madrid, 1948.

Flynn, Frederick E. *Wealth and Money in the Economic Philosophy of St. Thomas*. Notre Dame, Ind., 1942.

158   Bibliography

Gestoso y Pérez, José. *Sevilla Monumental y Artística.* 3 vols. Seville, 1889–92.

Gordon, B. Le Roy. *Human Geography and Ecology in the Sinu Country of Colombia.* Berkeley, 1957.

Gould, Alice B. "Nueva lista documentada de los tripulantes de Colón." *Boletín de la Academia de la Historia* (Madrid), vol. 110 (1942), 91–161.

Hamilton, Earl J. *American Treasure and the Price Revolution in Spain.* Cambridge, Mass., 1934.

Handbook of South American Indians. Vol. IV. New York, 1963.

Harrisse, Henry. *Discovery of North America.* London-Paris, 1892.

Journal of Christopher Columbus. Ed. Louis-André Vigneras. London, 1960.

Lane, Frederick C. *Venice and History.* Baltimore, 1966.

Magnaghi, Alberto. *Amerigo Vespucci.* Rome, 1926.

Martínez-Hidalgo, José María. *Columbus' Ships.* Barre, Mass., 1966.

Medina, José Torribio. *El Veneciano Sebastián Caboto al servicio de España.* 2 vols. Santiago, Chile, 1908.

Mercado, Tomás de. *Summa de Tratos y Contratos.* Seville, 1571.

Monetarius (Münzer), Hieronymus. "Itinerarium Hispanicum." Ed. Ludwig Pfandl. *Revue Hispanique,* vol. 48 (1920).

Montalboddo, Francesco. *Paesi novamente ritrovati.* Princeton, 1916.

Morison, Samuel Eliot. *Admiral of the Ocean Sea.* New York, 1942.

———. *Journals and Other Documents on the Life and Voyages of Christopher Columbus.* New York, 1963.

———. *Portuguese Voyages to America.* Cambridge, Mass., 1940.

Muro Orejón, Antonio. "La primera capitulación con Vicente Yañez Pinzón." *Anuario de Estudios Americanos,* vol. 4 (1947), 743–56.

Navarrete, Martín Fernández de. *Colección de los Viajes y descubrimientos que hicieron por mar los Españoles. . . .* 5 vols. Madrid, 1825–37.

Nunn, George E. *The Geographical Conceptions of Columbus.* New York, 1924.

O'Brien, George. *Essay on Medieval Economic Teaching.* London, 1920.

O'Gorman, Edmundo. *La Idea del descubrimiento de América.* Mexico City, 1951.

Ortega, Angel. *La Rábida*. 4 vols. Seville, 1925.

Oviedo y Valdés, Gonzalo Fernández de. *Historia general de las Indias*. 5 vols. Ed. Juan Pérez de Tudela. Madrid, 1955.

Pacheco Pereira, Duarte. *Esmeraldo de Situ Orbis*. London, 1937.

Parsons, James J. "Santa María la Antigua del Darién." *Geographical Review*, vol. 50 (1960), 294–96.

Pleitos de Colón. CDIU, vols. VII and VIII.

Pohl, Frederick Julius. *Amerigo Vespucci, Pilot Major*. London, 1966.

Polo, Marco. *Travels*. Ed. L. F. Benedetto. Transl. Aldo Ricci. London, 1950.

Ptolemy, Claudius. *Geographia*. Transl. E. L. Stevenson. New York, 1932.

Quirino de Fonseca, Henrique. *A Caravela Portuguesa*. Coimbra, 1934.

Ravenstein, Ernest George. *Martin Behaim, His Life and His Globe*. London, 1908.

Real Diaz, José. "El Sevillano Rodrigo de Bastidas." *Archivo Hispalense*, nos. 111–12 (1962), 61 ff.

Reichel-Dolmatoff, Gerardo. *Colombia*. New York, 1965.

Roukema, E. "Some Remarks on the La Cosa Map." *Imago Mundi*, vol. 14 (1959), 38–54.

Ruddock, Alwyn A. "John Day of Bristol and the English Voyages across the Atlantic before 1497." *Geographical Journal*, vol. 132 (1966), 225–33.

Sailing Directions for West Indies. 3rd ed. Vol. I. Washington, D.C.: Hydrographic Office (Pub. No. 21), 1958.

Sanuto, Marino. *Diarii*. 58 vols. Venice, 1879–1903. Vol. VI.

Sarabia de la Calle. *Instrucción de Mercaderes*. Medina del Campo, 1544; reprint, Madrid, 1949.

Sauer, Carl Ortwin. *The Early Spanish Main*. Berkeley, 1966.

Thacher, James Boyd. *Christopher Columbus*. 3 vols. New York, 1902.

Trevisan, Angelo. *Libretto de tutta la navigatione de Re de Spagna*. Paris, 1929.

Tumbo de los Reyes Católicos. Ed. R. Carande and J. de M. Carriazo. Seville, 1968—.

Vallés y Pujals, Juan. *Del Prestamo a interés*. Barcelona, 1933.

Vicens Vives, Jaime. *An Economic History of Spain*. Princeton, 1969.

Vignaud, Henry. *Toscanelli and Columbus*. London, 1902.

Vigneras, Louis-André. "Antecedentes familiares de Alonso de Hojeda." *Revista de Indias,* nos. 130–31 (1973).

————. "The Cape Breton Landfall: 1494 or 1497? Note on a Letter from John Day." *Canadian Historical Review,* vol. 38 (1957), 219–28.

————. The Cartographer Diogo Ribeiro." *Imago Mundi,* vol. 16 (1962), 76–83.

————. "El viaje de Esteban Gómez a Norte América." *Revista de Indias,* vol. 17 (1957).

Villalón, Cristóbal de. *Provechoso Tratado de cambios y contratación de mercaderes.* Valladolid, 1546.

Waldseemüller, Martin. *Cosmographiae Introductio.* Reprinted New York, 1907.

Washburn, Wilcomb. "The Meaning of Discovery." *American Historical Review,* vol. 68 (1962), 1–21.

Westropp, Thomas Johnson. "Brasil and the Legendary Islands of the North Atlantic." *Proceedings of the Royal Irish Academy,* vol. 30 (1912), section C, 223–60.

Williamson, James Alexander. *The Cabot Voyages and Bristol Discovery under Henry VII.* London, 1962.

Wittevroughel, Edouard. *De Nautico Foenore.* Dunkerque, 1895.

INDEX